THE GENTILE'S GUIDE

TO THE JEWISH WORLD

LEN CAVISE

Table of Contents

"What is Jewish and What is Goyish?"

(HERE'S AN OLD but timeless routine from Jewish comic Lenny Bruce. After reading it, you'll be able to update it on your own).

I'm Jewish. Count Basie's Jewish. Ray Charles is Jewish. Eddie Cantor's goyish. The B'nai Brith is goyish. Pumpernickel is Jewish and, as you know, white bread is very goyish. Instant potatoes – goyish. Black cherry soda's very Jewish. Macaroons are very Jewish. Fruit salad is Jewish. Lime Jello is goyish. Lime soda is very goyish. Trailer parks are so goyish that Jews won't go near them.

Balls are goyish. Titties are Jewish. Mouths are Jewish. All Italians are Jewish. Greeks are goyish. Eugene O'Neill – Jewish. Dylan Thomas – Jewish. Steve Allen is goyish, though. It's the hair. He combs his hair in the boys room with that soap all the time.

See how easy it is? Fidel Castro? Jewish – of course. Henry Kissinger – goyish. Marlon Brando – Jewish. Ringo is Jewish. Paul is goyish. John, of course, was Jewish.

Talk is Jewish. Silence is goyish. Thin is goyish. Fat is Jewish. Blue is Jewish. Green is goyish. Atheism is Jewish. Converting to Christianity is, of course, goyish. But, as R. Crumb points out, so is converting to Judaism. In fact, it's such a goyish thing, no Jew has ever done it.

Computers are Jewish. Rifles are goyish. California is goyish. France is Jewish. The thirties were Jewish. The forties were goyish. The fifties were goyish. The sixties were Jewish. The seventies were goyish. The eighties are off to an intensely goyisha start.

Ronald Reagan is goyish. Nancy Reagan is the most goyisha person who has ever lived. Marie Osmond is second. Tricia Nixon is third. Richard Nixon, however, was too much of an open maniac to be a goy.

OK, now you try it. One of the items in each pair listed below is Jewish, and the other one is goyish. Can you tell which is which?

Bowling alleys/constant guilt

Spam/chicken soup

Crew cuts/big, dark, almond-shaped eyes

Jumping out of planes/double-entry bookkeeping

Respecting your scoutmaster/believing you're Jesus Christ

INTRODUCTION

THIS BOOK IS not a typical travel book. I have only been to Israel as a short-term tourist and I have no idea where the best place is to stay in Jerusalem. I am a gentile, irretrievably gentile, who has lived in a largely Jewish world for many years.

In the United States, Jews comprise only three percent of the population. Worldwide, it's less than one percent. With numbers that small, who needs this book? Why not write a guide book to Armenian life since there are more Armenians then there are Jews? First, over 50% of all nice Jewish boys and girls are now intermarrying with gentiles. That's a lot of gentiles who need to learn what it means to sit *shiva* or to hide the *afikomen*. Second, Jewish words and expressions are everywhere. You need a phrase book and I'm happy to supply one. Third, everybody at some point, goes to New York and you don't need Lenny Bruce to tell you that New York is Jewish. So, if you want to sound like you're from the Midwest (and pay "special" prices), don't bother with this book. Fourth, and for many people this will be the most important, there is nothing wrong with learning enough about the history, religion, and language to avoid sounding like a total *goy* when you're invited somewhere Jewish.

The sad fact is that Jewish life is like a foreign culture to us gentiles. We know lots of Jewish celebrities and maybe even a few Jewish words but most of us are still lost at a *bar mitzvah* or when paying a condolence call at a Jewish home. What is appropriate to take to your hosts? Should I wear that "beanie" or not? Is it OK for me to sing that song too? What's the right thing to say on this particular occasion? It's kind of like going to a restaurant in Paris and you don't speak French. It may work out just fine and you might even enjoy yourself but everyone will know you don't have a clue. I'm here to help.

My Credentials

I WAS RAISED Italian Catholic in Upstate New York. I am the oldest of five children. My life was of many noisy people always arguing. Many Jews can identify with that. Eating was very important and just being Italian was important, even if we didn't always know what that meant. To us, all those WASPy people on the TV or in the papers ran the world but from somewhere else because we didn't see them in our world. And when it was time for girlfriends, the first question always was: is she a *paesan*?

I never really had an Italian girlfriend. They were all Jewish, including the one I've been married to for over forty years. Starting with the love of my high school life. I fell in love with her when I was a freshman. I memorized her schedule so that I could, just coincidentally, be outside her classroom where maybe she would say hello. I knew where her locker was so that I could change my routes around school and maybe bump into her. This went on for about, oh, three years – more or less. By the time we were seniors and I got up the courage to ask her out, I probably knew that she was Jewish but I don't remember how I came to that knowledge. I also can't think of any other Jewish kids in a graduating class of 427.

Ever since then, every serious girlfriend I've ever had (which really doesn't total all that many) was Jewish. This was not by design. I remember the night when the blond, University of Michigan sorority-girl *shikse* with the WASPy name let me play with a necklace around her neck and I saw it was the Star of David. When I asked what this was all about, I got the "I've been meaning to tell you" *spiel*, followed quickly by the "my parents say I shouldn't see you anymore" announcement. What got me is that we had been dating all summer and I didn't know. That scared me a little. By the time I met my eventual wife, Susan, I knew Kaplan to be a Jewish name and that her Jewishness was a good omen. That was in 1973. We've been together ever since. She has been my principal entrée into the Jewish world and, of course, my inspiration to write this book.

Susan was raised in a completely Jewish neighborhood on the

north side of Chicago. She was *Bat Mitzvah*ed and Sweet Sixteened and went to public schools that were mostly Jewish and Jewish summer camps and was in a Jewish sorority at the University of Wisconsin. All her boyfriends were Jewish. Unless I haven't been given full disclosure, it's my understanding that I was her first serious gentile boyfriend.

Susan's upbringing was Jewish in the sense that most of the family friends were Jewish. She went to temple but not regularly enough to qualify as a religious Jew. Her family was Conservative (see the chapter on religion). She went to countless Jewish weddings and funerals (by now, so have I). She always celebrates the High Holidays and Passover. Some of her fondest recollections are of Jewish holidays, like *Purim* where the kids have a party and make a lot of noise. Susan grew up thinking the whole world was Jewish. Before adulthood, she never set foot in a church and to this day doesn't really have any idea what Christianity is all about. And Protestants are a complete mystery to her. She wouldn't know a Baptist from a Lutheran. Perhaps most importantly, Susan is very funny and her humor is distinctly Jewish. Kind of Billy Crystal, with a touch of Sarah Silverman if you get my picture. In sum, if Susan knew anything about gentiles, she could write this book in her sleep.

Most of my closest friends are Jewish and some of them have read this book, including a Talmudic scholar and a rabbi, so you can trust me. It's now second nature to me to hate mayonnaise on deli meat and love *matzah* balls.

CHAPTER 1

SPEAKING JEWISH

The Phrase Book

JEWISH IS QUICKLY becoming the universal slang of the United States. Everyone is spicing up their language with Jewish words. Is there anyone who doesn't know what *shlep* means? As evidence of how far we have come, consider that people are suing people for using Jewish words. A restaurant in New York sued a guy who called their food "ground-up *shmutz*." Calling a building development a *"cockamamie* idea" landed one builder in Arizona in court. Saying that a business was a *"schlock* operation" cost somebody else attorneys' fees. The word *chutzpah* appears in over one hundred recently reported judicial decisions written by mostly gentile judges. Believe me, if the judges can get it, anybody can.

American Jews use Yiddish words. Not real Yiddish words but Yiddish words that have been adapted to fit into English or, better yet, American. Very few Jews alive today speak real Yiddish. Yiddish is not Hebrew, even though both are written from right to left. Hebrew is what people speak in Israel and in temple. Yiddish is the language of "the old country." It is a *bona fide* language, with grammar and style. There is a wealth of literature written in Yiddish. There's a Yiddish newspaper in New York that's been publishing for close to 100 years.

When the Jews first emigrated to America, Yiddish was the

dominant tongue. Over the generations it has been preserved in bits and pieces. What is used today is what I am calling "Jewish." "Jewish" is not a language. It represents more the art of spicing up your English with words taken from Yiddish roots but adapted for use in English. What follows is an attempt to communicate the basics of that art. Remember, if you can't say anything nice, say it in Jewish.

I have only included in this short dictionary those words that have most frequently crossed my path. My theory is that if I don't know the word after all these years, you don't need to know it either. Some New Yorkers may disagree on some points, but they always do. How's that for scientific?

Words that are used in cooking, religion, and Jewish ceremonies are more likely found in the chapters about those topics. I've included the pronunciation but keep in mind that, even in the U.S., there are regional differences. For example, in Pittsburgh, *mishpocha* is *mishpochee*.

How to use this vocabulary:[1]

**** *These are Jewish words or expressions that everyone should know*
*** *Useful and important words*
** *Words that are less useful and important but impressive nonetheless*
* *Words that separate you from the rest of the goyim*

Rating	Word	Meaning
*	alter kocker	an old man (usually a crochety old man). So, when all the old guys are sitting together, you can say "I'm going to go sit with the *alter kockers*."

---

1 Don't worry about my spelling. In researching this book, I have found that many Jewish words have more than one accepted spelling. Some of the most common variations: c tends to be used often instead of k.. And le is used often instead of q. Sh is sometimes used interchangeably with sch. And o is an ending sometimes when others would use er. So, if your favorite words are not being spelled here in the way that you would like it, just put in the spelling you use. Can you imagine having a Jewish spelling bee? Just imagine the lawsuits.

*	alva sholom	When gentiles refer to a departed friend by saying "may he (she) rest in peace," Jews say *alva sholom* softly, almost under their breath, whenever the name of the deceased is mentioned. If there are several Jews present, it could be a little chorus, like "Bernie, *alva sholom*, always use to say…." If somebody says it too loudly, they are making fun of the custom. Jews have a saying that you are never really dead until the last person who remembers you is dead, so this little custom can go on for quite a while.
**	*bissel*	a little bit. My nationality? I'm a *bissel* this, a *bissel* that….
***	*bobbe*	(pronounced bub-bee) This is used for an older lady, sometimes an affectionate name for a grandmother and a not-so-affectionate name for somebody who is acting older than they are.
**	bobeleh	(pronounced bubbela) affectionate term of endearment, especially among movie or theatre people. "I hate to say it, *bobeleh*, but you're through in this town."
***	bobbe-myseh	(bub-bee-my-sa) This means old wives tale, but usually silly or incredible. "That whole story was a big *bobbe-myseh*." Tie garlic around your neck to cure a cold and you'll know what an Italian *bobbe-myseh* is.
**	bubkes	(bub-kiss). Nothing. This is a great word. Comes from the Russian for "beans." It means you got nothing for your effort or your money. "And, for all that, what did she pay me? *Bubkes*." We'll talk about this later, but notice even here how

3

putting every "statement" into question form gives the "answer" so much more emphasis. In the above example, the "answer" "*bubkes*!" bangs onto the table of conversation. "What does he do during the day? *Bubkes*, that's what he does."

*	chozzerai	(haz-zair-eye). Junk or crap. Sometimes spelled really differently, like *chazerei.* "In that house, there was *chozzerei* everywhere." I come back from trips with nothing but *chozzerai.*
****	chutzpah	(hoots-pa: dont pronounce the c, spit the first h; don't pronounce the second one). Part of the beauty of Jewish words is that sometimes there is no equivalent in English. For this one, you can try the dull-sounding "wherewithal." Audacity, gall, guts and cajones also come to mind but they don't really make it. Leo Rosten defined *chutzpah* best: that quality in a person who, having killed both their mother and father, throws him or herself on the mercy of the court because he is an orphan.
**	cockamamie	(the second *a* is long). Crazy, foolish, incredible. This word might not be Jewish but it should be. "He told me some *cockamamie* story about getting held up by a pack of wild dogs."
**	cocked up	screwed up. Ruined. "He *cocked up* the whole plan.
***	drek	crap. Used to describe something distasteful; garbage. Be sure to emphasize it to get the full effect. "You eat that *drek*?"

*	farblondjet	(far-blun-jet) confused, totally lost. Another great emphasis word. "I turned the car around and got totally *farblondjet*.
*	farachadat	(usually mispronounced as *facockta*) crazy, confused, messed-up, or maybe just a lie. "If he ever gets here, he'll have some *facockta* story about where he was."
*	farshtinkener	(short i, accent the second syllable) rotten or stinking but not in the sense of odiferous. "That *farshtinkener* boyfriend of yours is making me crazy." This word is great for emphasis and for being uncouth without really sounding it.
**	fatootsed	All dressed up. I love this word (pronounced fatutsed – no "oo"). It's always an adjective. It saves having to say "dressed to the nines," or "dressed to kill," It sounds better anyway.
*	fermished	(accent second syllable) mixed up, lost, confused. "By the time he got to the point, I was totally *fermished*, with the point and the subpoint and the whole *facockta* thing."
*	fershtayst	always as a question. "Do you understand?" Somehow the Yiddish *verstehen* got changed to an f. In my ancestral tongue, it's just like "*capeesh*."
*	geh shlafen	(the *geh* is pronounced gay) This is a lovely way of saying "go to sleep." When used with children, it actually sounds like a good idea.
**	gesei gesund	(ga-zye-ga-zunt) This is a great one and very impressive. Literally, and when said sincerely, it means "go in good health" or "use it in good

health." Somebody might say it after you've just bought a car. It can also be used sarcastically, however, meaning "if that's the way you want it, so be it." In that case, the speaker is washing his or her hands of the whole thing. "You want to go to the Alps to go snowboarding, *gesei gesund*." Variations: *gaygezunt* or *gay gezunterhayt*.

*	geshrei	(geshr-eye) yelling, screaming, making noise (as in "stop *geshreing*").
**	gonif	a hustler, fast-buck artist, maybe even a thief. Usually applied to a dishonest or just overpriced merchant. For example, all used car salesmen are presumed *gonifs*.
****	good yuntiff	(or yontif). "Happy holiday." It's a salutation. Don't use it on *yom kippur*. That's not a happy holiday (see religion, later). Say it mostly on *Rosh Hashanah* (when L'shana Tova" is also used) or Passover.
**	gelt	Money. At *Hannukah*, those cute chocolate coins are called *Hannukah gelt*. Shekels is another common money word.
*	gornisht	(emphasize first syllable). Nothing. Great emphasis word, e.g. "I got *gornisht* out of that little deal." A lot like *bubkes,* but considerably more polite.
****	goy	a kind of pejorative way of saying gentile. Gentile is not actually a Yiddish word. *Goy* is like when some gentiles use the word "Jew" in a negative way. "A *goy* is always a *goy*." The plural is *goyim*. The adjective is as follows...

**	goyische	(goy-ish-a). This means *goy*-like. It applies to things as well as to people who are very un-Jewish. Very WASPy things (such as places, plays, food, law firms) are also very *goyishe*. White bread and mayonnaise are *goyishe*. In the introduction, I've reprinted a wonderful routine from Lenny Bruce (*alva sholom*) that really captures the essence of *goyishe* even though it's a little dated. If you want to be offensive, you can call something *goyishe* if it's stupid and only a *goy* would do it.
*	grepsing	hacking cough, choking, belching.
***	hock	to harass or badger someone. You *hock* somebody until they do it.
**	haimishe	(hay-mish-a) a warm, friendly, unpretentious home. It could also be descriptive of a person but not usually. It's a high compliment.
**	kepi	the head or the crown of the head, e.g. "watch out for your little *kepi*."
*	kinahora	(or kenahora) It's a little like "knock on wood," or "thank God" - may your good fortune continue. Its Yiddish roots were in warding off the evil eye or scaring away bad luck. You might say "my baby is in good health, *kinahora*."
****	kibbutz	a collective farm or settlement in Israel. People who live there are called *kibbutzim*. They date back to the founding days of Israel in the late 1940's but continue today as a major bulwark in the Israeli-Palestinian conflict.
****	kibbitz	The nice translation is to chat playfully But the classic example is the person who does a

running commentary on everybody else's moves at a card game. They don't really participate but they talk their way through everybody's business.

*** kibosh (short *I*, accent the second syllable) to put a stop to something. "He put the *kibosh* on that."

** klezmer traditionally, a small itinerant group of musicians. Now they're getting very hip and quite international.

**** klutz This one you also know. It means an awkward or clumsy person. Lots of people call themselves *klutzes*. It's not a very serious criticism.

** k'nocker a person who thinks they're a big shot, a braggart. Be sure to pronounce the "k."

**** kosher Literally, this means to eat under Orthodox Jewish laws. More traditional Jews will "keep *kosher*" in their home and in their eating habits. Some of the dietary rules that govern the *kosher* life are mentioned in the food chapter. The word is very versatile, however, as it sometimes refers to anything that's supposed to be on the up-and-up and legitimate. "Is what you're doing with the money *kosher*?" If you play by the rules, you're "keeping it *kosher*."

* kvell When your children do something you're really proud of or you're just extraordinarily pleased by something. "My son, he just got into medical school and I'm just *kvelling*."

**** kvetch one of the greatest words ever and you really should know it. It refers to a person who whines or complains or is constantly *kvetching* or is just "such a *kvetch*." It sounds so much better than the English. Be sure to include the k in your pronunciation or people will know.

* landsman (pronounce the first *a* like an *o* as in "lonsman") It used to mean somebody from your village but now it just means that the person referred to is Jewish.

**** l'chayim (luck-high-em. Spit the h). This is what you say when you toast just as you would say "to your health." It means "to life" in Hebrew.

*** macher (pronounced "mocker," accent the first syllable). Another word for big shot but this one is for a person who actually has made something of him or herself. "She's a big *macher* at the school." As opposed to the *k'nocker* who just thinks they're a big deal. You should learn this one.

* machetunim (pronounced mock-e-toon-em). These are the in-laws, the whole family.

*** maven (accent first syllable). Expert or connoisseur. "When it comes to French wine, Jack's the *maven*." Very useful compliment even if not always deserved.

**** mazeltov congratulations (in the sense of "you're having good luck"). You say *mazeltov* to the bride and groom; you say it when the baby is born or when somebody has an anniversary. It's a must-know. Jews only say "congratulations" when there are gentiles around, so separate yourself from that gentile crowd and say *mazeltov*.

*	megillah	the whole long story. It comes from the story of Esther which is a long complicated story that is read during the festival of *Purim*. "There, now you've got the whole *megillah*."

*** megillah

*** meshuga

(sometimes *meshugge, meshugga, meshugina, meshugenah* and oh so many other ways) It generally means senseless or crazy, idiotic. A person can be a *meshuga* - generally. "He's (or she's) a *meshuga*." "Stop acting like a *meshuga*." It can also be an adjective. "He (or she) had some *meshuggeneh* story like always." Or, in casual use, something like "you're one *mishugina* guy, but I love you, man." It gets thrown into a lot of conversations, so pay attention.

**** mensch

Definitely a must-know. A *mensch* is a very nice person, a real human being, either generally or in the moment. Do something nice for somebody, that makes you a *mensch* – for that moment. It's a very high compliment.

* mezuzah

a small object, normally just a couple of inches long, that you see on the right of the front door jamb that tells you that this is, or was, a Jewish household. Inside the *mezuzah*, there may or may not be a parchment with a prayer from Deuteronomy. The idea is that God will protect the house just like at Passover when the Jews marked their doors with lamb's blood, thus sparing their first born (see religious holidays, later). Some people wear *mezuzahs* as a charm, showing their pride. On the doorjamb, the *mezuzah* is hung at a slant because, it is said, the rabbis couldn't decide if it should be hung vertically or horizontally. So they compromised. Often, Jews will kiss the *mezuzah* as they enter or leave the house.

The Mezuzah

***	mishegoss	craziness, in general. "Let's avoid all the *mishegoss* and settle this right now.
****	mitzvah	a blessing, a kind act. Something just short of a miracle. Like the old Jewish joke: "20% off is a bargain; 50% off is a *mitzvah*."
***	moxie	Most people agree that this is not even a Jewish word. Having briefly studied the roots, it actually comes from Italian. It means that a person has balls, guts, pizzazz. It's a lot like *chutzpah* but it isn't as nervy. It's much more stylish.
*	naches	(pronounced knock-iss) It means the joy or happiness one gets from good fortune. You do something nice or do it well, you get a lot of *naches*. If you have nice kids, you get a lot of *naches* from them.
****	nebbish	The poor *nebbish*. Everybody feels bad for a *nebbish*. The *nebbish* is a weak, ineffectual, sometimes helpless person. You have heard this word
****	nosh	snacks or food to pick at. When you're *noshing*, you're not really eating and the calories don't count.
***	noudge	to bother, annoy, be pushy. "Stop *noudging* me. I'll leave when I'm ready."
**	nu?	This word has an infinity of uses. One possible translation: "So, what's happening? What's going to be?" The second: "I could have told you that." For example: "They just said it's going to rain tomorrow. *Nu?* It rains every day." Or, "the Alexa is listening to our conversations. *Nu?*"

The third: "So what have you got to say for yourself?" And fourth: it's a transition word for a conversation. Either, "let's change the subject" or "let's get back to the point. *Nu?*"

* ongeblozen   arrogant, conceited person

* ongepolchket   (but, pronounced, in its bastardized form oing-e-potch-kee). This can be an adjective or a verb. It means cluttered up or overdone. That house is all *ongeptochekeed*." Don't *ongepotchkee* everything. I love the word almost as much as I love *fatootsed*. It just says it all in one word.

**** oy   If you don't know this word, you have a lot of work to do. It's not really a word. It's an expression. Or, better yet, it's a state of mind. Though commonly heard as *oy vay* or even *oy gevalt*, it usually is enough to convey the sentiment of deep concern or frustration. As in much of the Jewish language, it's the only word necessary to show that you get just how serious this situation is or to describe just how you feel about it. The beauty of it is that *oy* stands alone. It doesn't need an explanation or more sentences of exactly what you mean. It does it all by itself.

** pisher   This is a great put-down; it's used to describe somebody who's too young, too inexperienced, or just too much of a nobody to count much. "Who is this little *pisher* to tell me where I can sit?" "Look at the little *pisher* he appointed to be a *macher* in the government!" The word "little" is usually a modifier. You have to be at least middle-aged to use this.

*	plotz	Collapsing (usually on a nice sofa) as if to take a load off. "All I want to do is *plotz* when I get home." Some people *plotz* in one place forever. Another use, though, is really cool: some people laugh so hard, they could just *plotz*. You know what the English word is. Obviously, popular usage has expanded its definition.
**	potchke	(pronounced "potchkey") A slap. Like "a *potchke* on the *tuches*," which is a slap on the butt. Again, this word has expanded dramatically to include a great expression like "I'm just going to *potchke* around this afternoon." As in "play around." Don't ask me how it got to that.
*	pupik	the belly button.
**	pulkees	thighs. Thighs you don't want unless you're a toddler. It really only deserves one * but if you hang around Jewish women at all, you'd be well served to know it.
**	putz	Used literally, it's really not nice. As slang, however, it's not nice but it's usable to describe a person who's a jerk. It just has a great sound; so much stronger- sounding than jerk.
*	rachmones	(pronounced rock-moan-us; spit the h) A convicted defendant would make a plea for *rachmones* to a judge. A plea for mercy, appealing to the kind of compassion that permeates Judaism.
***	shalom	Peace, hello, goodbye. *Shalom Aleichem*: peace be with you. *Shabbat shalom* is peaceful Sabbath.

*   shaygets   a male gentile but a pejorative way of saying it.

*   shayna punim   (this is actually two words but you'll rarely hear one without the other). Pretty face. Used mostly for babies and grandchildren except for *shayna maidela which means pretty girl.*

****   shiksa   This is a female *shaygets*. For some reason, this word is much better known than the male equivalent. Could there be a gender-based criticism to make of this Yiddish word? I don't think so. Any female who is not Jewish is a *shiksa* and that is from that.

****   shlep   to drag around, usually slowly. "You've been *shlepping* that thing around all day (as a verb). A *shlepper* (the noun) is one who *shleps* but is often used to refer to maladroit loser—types. It's worse than being called a plugger. "Who wants to go out with a *shlepper* like him?"

***   shlemiel   a loser – whether foolish or unlucky. Usually awkward as well. You can dislike a *shlemiel* whereas you feel sorry for a *nebbish.*

****   shlock   cheap stuff. A knock-off. Stores on *shmatte* row usually sell *shlock* stuff. A whole business can also be a *"shlock* operation." *Shlock* houses are run by *shlockmeisters.*

*   shlong   another not-so-nice word referring to male genitalia that doesn't really have another use.

*   shonda   a shame, scandal, or embarrassment

****   schmaltz   Another wonderful word that really doesn't have an English equivalent. As a verb: *schmaltz* it up. As an adjective, that's too *schmaltzy*. As a noun:

that was all *schmaltz*. Corny, over-sentimental or emotional are translations that come to mind. Whatever it is, *smaltz* means it's exaggerated. Literally, it's an animal fat that gets *shmeered* on a piece of bread.

**	shmatte	(or *schmatte*) literally, a rag. In common usage, it's an item of clothing that the speaker does not think is pretty, as in "this old *shmatte*." It comes from Polish but has totally been adopted. "*Shmatte* row is a way of referring to strip malls that sell discount clothes.
*	shmendrick	another pejorative word used to describe a person, like *shlmiel*, *shmageggie* and *nebbish*. Bumbling and incompetent, as in "I'm working for a bunch of *shmendricks*. This one carries with it the notion of jerkiness, kind of like *pisher* but you don't have to be young.
*	shmie	(pronounced sh-my) to wander without a particular goal. "I went to the mall and just *shmied* around."
****	shmooz	You must know this one. It means to hang out or, as the Brits would say, to chat with someone. "Go *shmooz* him up." "He's a great *shmoozer*."
****	shmuck	Used literally, it's another one that has to do with male genitalia. As slang, you know what this means.
***	shmutz	Dirt, or a stain, but it can apply to any kind of spot that shouldn't be there. "You've got *shmutz* on your tie."

**	shnook	Are you getting tired of all these not-nice "sh" words? This is another person to be pitied, rather than disliked. The *shmuck* is the one you dislike.
**	shnorrer	a moocher or somebody who's really cheap. "Don't be a *shnorrer*, put in five bucks." Traditionally, it was a beggar. It's another great word because it kind of says it all.
***	shnoz	nose
**	shpritz	a spray, a little taste. Can be a verb or a noun, e.g. give me a *shpritz* of that stuff; that cat is *shpritzing* all over the house.
****	shtik	You have to know this too but it's hard to define. It's somebody's routine or their "thing." You could have a general *shtik* or just a particular one that you like to do. "He does that same *shtik* at every party."
**	shtunk	a mean, nasty, disagreeable person.
***	shtup	This is the Jewish equivalent of the "f" word except that you don't say "*shtup* you."
*	shul	the temple or synagogue
*	shvartzeh	another not nice word but its equivalent probably exists in all languages. It's the Jewish word for Black person coming from the Yiddish word for black. Definitely used pejoratively. Don't say it but know it when you hear it.
***	shvitz	This is just a great alternative for the word "sweat." "I've been *shvitzing* all day.
**	spiel	usually refers to an oral presentation of some story. "He gave me his whole *spiel*." It's not the

same as somebody's *shtik* which refers more to style than to substance. When you give a *spiel* about something, you aren't necessarily doing *shtik*. But you could be.

** shpilkes

(pronounced shpilkeys) to have the *spilkes* is to have the butterflies or to be anxious. Little Richard (who, by the way, was Jewish, called it the "Heebie Jeebies"). This is an important word for many Jews (perhaps the majority, according to one study) who already have a tendency to be anxious in general. One author says, in a 2012 interview, that this tendency comes from the *Talmudic* tradition of constant, interminable questioning and turning things over and over and analyzing and reanalyzing.[2] Others say it's because Jews have always felt a little alien, given the many centuries of anti-Semitism and this feeling causes them constant anxiety. In any event, everybody get the *spilkes* at least once in awhile.

* shtetl

This was the Jewish part of town back in the old country. It was usually what we now call a ghetto. An enormous percentage of American Jews trace their ancestry back to these Jewish quarters in Eastern Europe where Jewish culture and religion thrived. Most were destroyed by *pogroms* which were anti- Semitic attacks led by modern versions of the Huns.

*** tchotchke

(don't pronounce the "t" – it's chachkee). Knick-knacks or other little, inexpensive things. Some

---

2 See Smith, Daniel, "Monkey Mind: A Memoir of Anxiety,"

people have *tchotchkes* all over the house. Some stores are *tchotchke* joints.

** tsouris (pronounce the "t" but mainly as a grace note for the "s"). It means aggravation or trouble. "Oy, have I got *tsouris*." "You don't have children? What do you do for *tsouris*?"

*** tuchis (pronounced took-us, accent first syllable) This is the rear end, the derriere. A particularly cute baby gets "*potchkeed* in the *tuchis*" all the time.

* ver vayst (or Wer Weiss) It means who knows?

*** yenta a gossip, a woman who meddles in other people's business, a busybody. Always a woman. In Fiddler on the Roof, the *yenta* was also a match-maker. There's no reason why this couldn't also apply to men, except tradition. Tradition unhampered by progress.

** yontiff (pronounced yun-tiff) Good *yontiff* means good holiday. Don't say it on *Yom Kippur*.

* zayde (pronounced zay-dee, accent first syllable). A male *bubbee*. An old guy or grandfather.

* zaftig most often used as an adjective to describe a buxom, plump or just plain overweight female. Comes from the Yiddish meaning "juicy" or "succulent." I don't make this stuff up.

*** zhlob (pronounced zhlub). A really gross, insensitive, ill- mannered, probably not so good-looking guy. Usually a guy. Any male who is substantially overweight is in danger of being called a *zhlob*.

THE TEN COMMANDMENTS
OF USING JEWISH WORDS

1. **Never talk Jewish with food in your mouth**. So many of the words are guttural that I have often wound up spitting on my dinner partners. If you don't spit just a little, you're probably saying the word wrong. If you try to say "this is great *challah*" with *challah* in your mouth, you're probably not Jewish.

2. **Never talk Jewish when you can't use your hands or appropriate body parts**. Conversation is an art that requires more than just the mouth. We all know about talking with our hands, particular when emphasis is needed. Italians are gifted at using the hands to touch the bottom of the eye or to swipe the back of the hand through the chin or grasp the inner part of the elbow to communicate just how much you feel what you are saying. Many of those hand gestures are so common as to not require any words at all. Jews are pretty good at the hand signaling as well but they are positively distinguished when it comes to head movements. Many things, for example, are not to be spoken out loud and therefore require a lot of eye rolling and head-nodding. If the sentence starts "let's just put it this way…" you can be sure that you are about to see a great head move and then, if you're lucky, you'll be cut in on some information that just can't be spoken.

3. **Never ask for grammatical help**. Yiddish has grammar. Jewish doesn't. Once you get the root word, don't worry about verb forms, plurals, etc. It all follows English. The past tense of *shlep* is *shlepped*. One who *shleps* is a *shlepper*. The plural of *shlepper* is a bunch of *shleppers*. *Hock* is a verb. You *hock* somebody. When they're sick of being *hocked*, they say stop *hocking* me.

4. **Never try to make a sentence out of Jewish words**. These words are meant to be used freestanding. The rest of the sentence is English. The Jewish word is there for clarity or emphasis. "She's got a lot of *chutzpah*." Never hide these words in a sentence. In fact,

organize your thought around the word. Their beauty is that they highlight nicely. *"Goniffs. That's what they are. Goniffs."* Or, "I don't want to hear the whole *spiel*." See how the whole sentence is weighted toward the Jewish word?

5. **Never try to pronounce the Jewish word the way it is in the original Yiddish**. Most of these words are heavily mutated to suit Jewish American needs. Since most of us are linguistically challenged, we tend to simplify, mispronounce and misuse as necessary. That's what's happened to modern Jewish. For example, in Yiddish, the word is *nebech* but everybody says *nebbish*. A Jewish friend of mine congratulated me on saying *Tor-ah'* instead of *Tor'-ah* which is how everybody else says it. I want to be like everybody else and not be a show-off, so I opted to say it the way everybody does.

6. **Never use your advanced Jewish words in a primarily gentile crowd**. An advanced Jewish word is any word with fewer than four stars in the accompanying glossary. They won't get it. You might as well be speaking Greek. I am amazed at how many people still do not know what *shlep* means or *mishigoss*. They look at each other as in "did I miss something?" or "was that an ethnic reference?" They won't even get it if you're faking actually *being* Jewish *for* those many situations where it's an advantage, like when you're auditioning to be a law professor.

7. **Never be timid about using Jewish words**. The first time I use a word is always a little risky. Jews may even giggle a little. But that's only the first time. From then on, you own the word.

8. **Never stop the conversation cold to show off your Jewish words**. Don't say, "You know what this is? It's a *mitzvah*." Don't say, "You know what kind of a guy he is? He's a *mensch*." Nobody likes a show-off, especially a gentile one. You just put the word in the conversation as though it's the easiest, most effective, and, sometimes, the most colorful way of saying what you want to say. "That guy's a real *mensch*." Or, "that was a very *mensch*-like thing to do." No big

deal. Then watch all the Jews smile or even say "Are you sure you're not Jewish?" This, of course, is the ultimate compliment.

9. **Never mix Jewish with another language or dialect**. Your thought loses all meaning and everybody will know that you're just showing off which, everybody knows, the *goyim* love to do. So, don't say "hey, *que pasa*, you old *schlemie*l!

10. **Never try to cover up a linguistic mistake**. When corrected, I used to say "Oh, that's how I've always heard it pronounced," or "maybe it's a New York thing." Nobody ever believed me, no matter how sincere I was. Remember, everybody makes mistakes, even Jews. I once heard a Jew say "You bet!" And another one who said "darn right I do!" But this happened in Iowa and maybe they were doing Iowa shtik and I caught them in the act.

HOW TO ANSWER
QUESTIONS WITH QUESTIONS

People who aren't Jewish are accustomed to having answers follow questions. That's why we say we're going to have a "Q and A session." That why they have scantron tests and multiple-choice questions. If you have a question, there's almost always some kind of appropriate answer to it. Even when the answer is "I don't know," there has at least been a response to the question that may or may not be dispositive.

What we gentiles don't know is that to actually answer a question is a strategic decision. Why should you answer a question? Did the question deserve an answer? The question was so good, I have to answer it? What do I look like, some guy on Jeopardy?

You want me to tell you why you don't have to answer the question? I'll tell you why you don't have to: because, in Jewish, the question is usually more important than the answer. Nobody cares about your answer, Mr. Know-it-All. Maybe it's not time yet for an answer. This is very hard to learn and you must be patient with yourself. Please don't take it personally when you have a solution – an answer, as it were – and nobody is listening. It's not that they don't like your answer or that they don't like you. In, for example, academic circles, it is the question that must be appreciated and finely simmered until it's just right. Like a fine wine, there shall be no answers before their time. First, we have to ask questions for a while. Like the Four Questions at Passover. Does anybody call them the Four Answers? Does anybody even know (without looking) what the answers are to the Four Questions?

Answering a question with another question serves a second more strategic purpose. It's a cover when you just don't know the answer. It's an aggressive, self-affirming way of responding when a gentile would maybe hang his or her head and simply take their lumps.

Q. What is the capital of Kentucky?
A. How would I know the capital of Kentucky? Who's even heard of Kentucky?

Q. What's your solution to global warming?
A. Is it really a good idea to separate this question from the other questions? Has it really come to that?

That is what we mean when we say the best defense is a good offense. Totally delegitimize the question and affirm that you have too much self-respect to trouble your mind with meaningless details. People who answer questions with questions probably have more self-esteem.

Answering with a question is also a common way to say "yes." But, if done right, it says yes with enthusiasm and *moxie*.

Q. Do you want to go see that movie?
A. Do I want to see it? Have I been waiting to see it since it came out?
Q. Do you like George Clooney?
A. Do I like George Clooney? Do I look blind to you?
Q. Did you like that book?
A. Did I like that book? Did I get no sleep for three nights because of that book?

The question technique is also very useful even when no question has been asked, as a means of putting back into question something that already appears decided.

Q. Dad, I'm going to Florida over spring break.
A. For this I'm spending fifty thousand a year?
Q. I need some cash for the trip.
A. What am I, a money tree?
Q. I'm taking my girlfriend with.
A. What, are you trying to give me a heart attack?

HOW TO MAKE ENGLISH SOUND LIKE JEWISH

The problem with using English words in a way that actually sounds Jewish is that of tone and cadence and volume. For a Jewish person, a sentence has a certain song to it. Imagine Billy Crystal or Sarah Silverman throwing up their hands and saying, "I should only live so long" or a Jewish mother saying "what, you couldn't call?" The language drips with sarcasm and *schmaltz*. Even if we had audiotapes to accompany this book, we couldn't teach you how to sing Jewish. Gentiles who try to sing like Jews are considered, at best, cute. Jews know it doesn't come naturally to you so they figure you're just putting it on to make an impression.

Here are a few English words or parts of words (in sample context) whose usage is important in Jewish not so much for what they mean but for how they are used and with what kind of emphasis – in just the right places. Sometimes they're used to be sarcastic, sometimes just to emphasize how strongly you feel, sometimes to show just how bored you are with this whole conversation. If I thought I could teach you to how to use these types of words, I would. But I really can't. You decide if you can pull it off without getting the condescending smile.

Already	*So, get to the point already* *Enough already!*
Better	*better you than me* *Better you should go or he'll hock you all day*
By	*by me, that's too much* *That, by you, is a good deal?*
Know from	*She doesn't know from baseball*
Make	*let's make a party or a wedding or any celebration*
So?	*So, your point is?* *So, I should say I'm sorry to that* shmuck? *So, sit and stop kvetching.*

Should	*You should only live so long*
	You should be that smart
	I'm sorry. I should go throw myself in front of a truck?
	I should pay that goniff those prices?
Such	*such a nice boy. Is he married?*
	Such an important man. You should only be that important.

Then, there are a few Jewish suffixes that are added to English words that you should probably learn to recognize. Such as:

-chik	It's a diminutive. My *boychik* is my darling little boy.
-ele	An affectionate diminutive. "Where's my little *dollele*?" My little Suzele?
-nik	Part of or relating to a group. A *nudnik* is a dummy. Remember "peaceniks?" "Beatniks?" "Refusniks?"
shm-	This is actually a prefix. It's usually a sign of disagreement, contempt or at least a put-down.
	"Hurry, shmurry, I'm taking my time."
	"Harvard, shmarvard, he's still a *putz*."
	"Oedipus, shmedipus, so long as he loves his mother. "
	"Bill, shmill, what does he know?"

GET THE IDEA?

There are also numbers of popular English expressions that are frequently used by Jews. They probably come directly from Yiddish sayings. I'm not sure but I have my suspicions.

Knock on wood

I need that like I need a hole in the head

From your lips to God's ears

I don't want to say anything, but....

Don't ask! (This is a standard answer to any question that begins: "How's your....")

Use it in good health

From that he makes a living?

God forbid....

What am I, chopped liver? (definitely depassé)

THE ART OF JEWISH CONVERSATION OR HOW TO TALK FOR 30 MINUTES ABOUT WHERE YOU PARKED THE CAR

The purpose of this section is not to suggest that Jewish conversation is mundane or frivolous. Not at all. The idea is that, no matter how mundane the topic, Jewish conversation exhibits a unique dynamic, a vibrancy, a certain *je ne sais quoi*. Just look at the examples.

The gentile conversation upon arrival at an event:

"It was very difficult to park anywhere near here."

"I know what you mean. I had trouble finding the place and the parking around here is very confusing."

The Jewish conversation at the same event:

"I'm totally exhausted. You have no idea what we had to do to get here. I'm amazed we're here. For awhile I thought we were going to end up in *outer Kishinev* [it's a place far away, nobody knows where – you just say it]"

"Did he try the lot? I told him to try the lot but, no, he had to park a mile away, we're late and I'm *shvitzing* through my dress."

You don't know what bad is. Did you spend an hour circling the place on an empty tank of gas and she has to go to the bathroom?"

"What! An hour! God forbid they should have valet parking in this place. Who needs this *tsouris*? For a couple of bucks, you give it to the guy and that's it."

Not to mention there's no lights around here. I'm driving around in the dark, can't read the directions and can't see where I'm going. I thought I was going to *plotz*.

Don't start with me on the directions. Who wrote those directions? You have to have a master's degree to understand them. *Oy*, the things you go through in this life."

It's just a beautiful thing to witness that conversation. You notice the gift for hyperbole that is evident in the Jewish conversation. What I can't reproduce is the speed, cadence, and the collective spirit of the conversation. By collective spirit, I mean simply that everybody is involved and, if it's really good, everybody is interrupting or just talking over everybody. Now that's a good conversation! I remember the time that there were six of us, I was the only gentile, and the other five were all talking at the same time. And it worked. If it's just your monologue, people are undoubtedly bored. As author Molly Katz says to gentiles who marry into Jewish families, in *Jewish as a Second Language*: "By now you've had at least twenty years in which to finish your sentences. This is enough for anybody. We hope you enjoyed the luxury while you had it, because you'll never finish one again."

WHAT IS JEWISH GEOGRAPHY AND HOW DO YOU PLAY IT?

Most people think Jewish geography is nothing more than a game of "Who Do You Know?" But that's not really true. The game is not to show off the important people you know or the trivia you know about them or even to discuss the people you have in common with someone. The game is used as a means for two people to get to know each other. Tell me whom you have known in your life and I will tell you who you are.

If you're not Jewish, my advice is very simple. Don't play. Unless you're a gentile who grew up in a Jewish neighborhood, joined a Jewish club or sorority or whatever in college or went into a business where there are a lot of Jews, you just can't hope to hold up your end of the game for more than a minute or two and you'll be frustrated. Gentiles simply lack the database from which to retrieve a good game, and they don't know the rules. The object of the game, again, is nothing less than to figure out who this person is you're playing with. One good game of Jewish geography and you know pretty much everything you need to know about your playing partner.

The game is not about the people you are naming. Who those people are couldn't be more irrelevant. They're only the stepping-stones to the next space in the game. The game is about the players. When gentiles discuss with each other whom they know in common, they tend to linger on the things they know about the person whose name has turned up on the board. In Jewish geography, that's totally unimportant. What is important is whom you know NEXT. The beauty of the game is that you never know where it'll take you. How deep into the recesses of repressed memory will you have to go to keep up your end? Who will be the first one to mention somebody nobody knows? When will you hit the dead end? Good game or bad game, you'll always know it's over when somebody says: "small world."

Here's an example. First, two gentiles are talking:

> *Chip: Oh, you went to Michigan. Did you know a Maggie Smith?*
>
> *Bill: Why, yes I did. Kind of short girl with curly hair? Yeah, she was in the same residence hall one year. How did you know her?*
>
> *Chip: I dated her when we were in high school.*
>
> *Bill: Oh. She was a nice kid. I remember she used to like folk music a lot.*
>
> *Chip: She did? I guess I didn't know that. I only dated her for a while. We used to go to the movies and stuff like that.*
>
> *Bill: Yeah, well, small world.*

Ok, that was a terrible game. Now let's have Barry and Bernie play the same game, using the same data base:

Barry: You went to Ann Arbor. Did you know Maggie Smith?

Bernie: Did I know Maggie Smith? She was only in the next hall from me freshman year. How do you know her?

Barry: Unbelievable. She was my senior year girlfriend in high school.

Bernie: No way. What high school did you go to?

Barry: Lakeland. I'm trying to think who went to Michigan. Did you know Steve Schwartz?

Bernie: He was two years ahead of me. I knew his brother Phil. He went to Michigan too. You must have known him at Lakeland.

Barry: I didn't know him but I knew their cousin Mike Schwartz.

Bernie: The one who went to Downstate and got busted for dope?

Barry: Everybody knew him. His roommate is the one who went to Hollywood, wrote a script and made a million dollars.

Bernie: Yeah. He went out with Maggie Smith too.

This game could have gone on forever. Once again, you get the idea.

CHAPTER 2

HOW TO ONE UP YOUR JEWISH FRIENDS

ELEMENTARY JEWISH HISTORY

STUDYING HISTORY, WITHOUT special effects, is boring. That's why we have painting, music, television, Hollywood and cyberspace. For Christians, studying history, particularly the history of Christianity, has always been easier. After all, wasn't historical Christianity the primary subject for the Renaissance painters? Sculptors? Musicians? Name five great works of fine art after Christ and before 1700 that were not Christian in character or subject matter. OK, the Mona Lisa is one. Name four more. Now name five great Jewish artists, composers or sculptors from the same time period. This is not to say that there were no great Jewish artists during all of this time but, clearly, most of their work was clandestine, destroyed, or the notes were simply not written down. Only a few writings remain. After 1700, political history and religious history separated but both remained hot subjects for visualization. Still, Jewish history was not part of the curriculum.

At the risk of making this book seem a little too like an "Idiot's Guide," the task falls to me to trace the history of the Jewish people in a hopefully light-hearted way that discusses the questions that you want to know, mindful, as always, that there may not be answers. You will note that many Jews do not know this history because they did not go to Hebrew school and the *Talmud* was not required reading in public schools. For those reasons, I will try to cut to the chase and assume practically nothing.

Frequently Asked Question No. 1:
What is the Jewish take on the Bible and Jesus Christ?

There is a simple answer to this bottom-line question. The first five books of the Old Testament of the Bible are the same for Jews and Christians. Burning bush, Moses, Ten Commandments, Genesis – the whole nine yards is exactly the same. Jews and Christians differ on the New Testament which dates from the birth of Christ. Jews don't believe in the New Testament or in Jesus Christ as God or the Messiah. Jews recognize Christ as a Jewish teacher or leader but the gospels of Mathew, Mark, Luke and John are not recognized in the Jewish religion.

Frequently Asked Question No. 2:
Why Do the Jews Call Themselves the "Chosen People?"

In about 1700 B.C., Abraham made a deal (a "covenant") with God that, as long as Abraham and his family tow the line and obey God, Abraham would be the father of a great people that would always have a special, a chosen relationship to God. Part of the deal was that all Jewish males would be circumcised "in the flesh of your foreskin." *Ergo*, the *bris* – to be discussed later. Abraham had 12 sons, each of whom begat one of the twelve "tribes" of Israel.

There is another reason why Jews (except the Reconstructionists whom I describe in the religion section) call themselves the chosen people. According to scripture, God gave the *Torah* (the name for the Jewish Bible) to Moses, a Jew, and Moses accepted it. This doesn't mean that Jews have a religious superiority complex. In fact, the Prophets say that God offered the *Torah* to all people and only the Jews would accept it. Because of that, they gained special status in the eyes of God (Deuteronomy 332, Habakkuk 33). Quoting God (not sure how you do that), the Prophet Amos declared: "You alone have I singled out of all the families of the earth. That is why I will call you to account for all your iniquities."

Frequently Asked Question No. 3:
What Exactly was the Exodus All About?

This takes a little explaining. In about 1500 B.C., the twelve tribes emigrated from Canaan (the Promised Land of Israel) to Egypt on the invitation of Joseph, one of Abraham's sons. Things went well for a time but, eventually, Pharaoh saw the Jews as a political threat and tried to reduce their numbers by limiting the opportunity to procreate. First, he made them work 16 hours a day making bricks to build the pyramids. The Jews kept having children. Then, he separated the husbands and wives but, by subterfuge, the wives managed to make visits and make more children. Then, the Pharaoh decided to kill all the male Jewish infants and have the midwives tell the Jewish mothers that their children had been stillborn. When he realized that many of the midwives were secretly saving the babies, he ordered all Egyptians to kill every newborn Israelite child.

Jocheved, a Jewish mother, hid her child until he became too active. She put him in a basket and had her daughter, Miriam, take the basket to the Nile and watch over it. Pharaoh's childless daughter found the basket. Miriam revealed herself and asked the princess if she would like a Hebrew nurse. That's how Jocheved became the nurse for her own child in the court of Pharaoh. And the child was named Moses.

Eventually, Jocheved tells Moses that he's an Israelite (the term Jewish wasn't even used until after the Exodus) and she never let him forget it. When, as a young man, Moses visited the Israelites out in the fields making bricks, he saw a man being whipped. Moses is enraged, kills the slave master on the spot, and then goes immediately into exile.

One day, while tending sheep, Moses spotted a burning bush and he started hearing things – his name, in particular. God appeared and told Moses to negotiate with Pharaoh for the release of the Jews from Egypt. Moses started up with Pharaoh who was stubborn but Moses persisted. This leads us to the story of the Ten Plagues.

Moses told Pharaoh that plagues would hit Egypt. The first plague would turn the Nile into blood. Pharaoh refused to let the Jews go, so for seven days, there was blood everywhere and everybody was digging elsewhere for water. The second plague was frogs everywhere – in the food, the house, the clothes. Pharaoh gave in and the frogs withdrew but then Pharaoh reneged on his agreement. The third plague was lice, the fourth swarming flies. Again, Pharaoh relented but then changed his mind. The fifth killed all the livestock, the sixth was painful skin boils on everyone, the seventh was hail, thunder and lightning that killed everything outdoors. Again Pharaoh relented and changed his mind. The eighth was locusts everywhere, the ninth was a dark fog across the whole country and the tenth was the killing of every firstborn child and animal in every home.

On the night of the tenth plague, God told Moses to have the Jews pack their bags to leave. He also instructed them to slaughter a lamb and mark the doorposts with its blood so that the Angel of Death would "Passover" the house. When Pharaoh lost his only child, he ordered Moses to take the Jews out of Egypt immediately. The *Torah* says 600,000 Jews left that night with everything they could carry, including the unleavened bread. They were in a hurry. Who had time to wait for the bread to rise?

When, again, Pharaoh – definitely a slow study – changed his mind and sent the soldiers after the Israelites, a strong wind parted the Red Sea, allowing the Jews to cross. The water then closed on the soldiers. Maybe you've seen this scene in a classic movie called Exodus. It's truly spectacular which is why a Hollywood director named Cecil B. DeMille made millions.

In sum, the flight from Egypt is the Exodus. The holiday of Passover (see description later) is celebrated to commemorate the *Exodus*.

Frequently Asked Question No. 4:
How did the Jews Wind up in Israel?

To pick up our story, Moses led the Jews out of Egypt into a desert. At a hill called Mount Sinai, God gave the Jewish people, through Moses, the *Torah* and the Ten Commandments. There's an old Jewish joke that says that Moses came down from the mountain and told his people: "I have good news and bad news. The good news is that I got him down to ten. The bad news is that adultery is still in."

So, the Jews wandered in the desert for forty years before they reached the promised land, Canaan (which they had left about 150 years earlier). They had to re-conquer it. Each tribe received a portion of land upon arrival; they organized themselves into a loose federation of the twelve tribes and eventually into one kingdom. About 1000 B.C., the first famous king – Solomon – built the first temple in Jerusalem. When Solomon died, the kingdom split into two rival groups, one based in Samaria and called Israel, and one called Judah with the capital in Jerusalem. They were eventually both destroyed and the tribes dispersed. Throughout early history, groups of Jews returned to Israel to observe what they thought was a commandment of the Torah. The second temple was built and destroyed by the eventual conquerors – the Romans. Here the story takes an important twist. To be continued.

Frequently Asked Question No. 5:
Did the Jews Really Kill Jesus?

The great Jewish comedian, Lenny Bruce, once said, as part of his nightclub stand-up *shtick*:

All right. I'll clear the air once and for all, and confess. Yes, we did it. I did it, my family. I found a note in the basement. It said "We killed him. Signed, Morty."

Never one to hesitate jumping in way over my head, let me resolve a question has troubled Biblical scholars and theologians for centuries. The Jews did not kill Jesus. Pontius Pilate did. He was Roman, a forefather of my very own Italian *compadres*. Now, some will say that the Jews *wanted* Christ killed, so here's the story.

A group called the Pharisees dominated Judaism in the first century but there were, at the time, several different Jewish sects. When the Romans conquered Judea, the Pharisees worked out a deal with the conquerors whereby they would cooperate without conforming to Roman culture in exchange for limited religious sovereignty. In other words, they paid taxes and obeyed the Roman emperors but did not worship him.

Jesus, probably raised as a Pharisee but definitely a lifelong Jew, was the charismatic leader of a group of Jewish troublemakers. It's open to question whether Christ actually intended to split from Judaism and form Christianity. It's open to question whether he actually knew who he was or what his role was to be. That's why he went to the desert for 40 days and 40 nights, asking: "Who do you say I am?" For this reason, many Jewish scholars say that not even Jesus saw himself as the Savior or Messiah. Some say he was just rabble-rousing, trying to revitalize Judaism by criticizing the politicians and their hypocrisy wherever he saw it. Either way – Messiah or revolutionary – he was not a bad guy.

Jesus definitely broke with the party line and was therefore *persona non grata* to the ruling Jewish hierarchy. But it was the Romans who killed him because they didn't want him and his followers threatening Roman rule. Times were very tense and there was a delicate political balance to be maintained so it's doubtful that the Pharisees much regretted the whole pageant of Jesus' execution.

Not everybody agrees with the above analysis. The New Testament implies that Pontius Pilate was so weak that he bowed to Jewish pressure to kill Christ. At one point, the Book of Mathew even says that the Jews *delivered* Christ to Pilate who was unwilling to condemn Jesus and who "washed his hands" in public to remove Christ's blood. Other historical records say, however, that Pilate was a brutal and bloodthirsty ruler who consulted no one on crucifixions, which was the preferred Roman method of execution. Only if one believes that powerful Jewish leaders persuaded a weak Pilate to prosecute Christ does it figure that the Jews could be co-conspirators at most. In any event, Pilate ordered the crucifixion. That scene in the movies where the crowd chants for Christ to be killed and for the thief Barabbas to be saved is apocryphal, as are many of the tracts of the New Testament, much of which wasn't even written until hundreds of years later.

There you have it, the straight story. But, old ideas die hard and, even today, the world's most famous passion play, the 400 year old *Oberammergau* continues to portray the Jews (sometimes in horned costumes) as the Bad Guys fighting against Christ who represents Absolute Good, with old Pilate sitting around in the white gown of the Innocent.

How did this conflict end? Christ's followers dispersed into the gentile world. Only the Pharisees survived the destruction of the second temple in 70 A.D. Exile led the others to what are now Central Europe, Ethiopia, Italy, Spain and North Africa.

Frequently Asked Question No. 6: Is it True that Everybody is Always Trying to Wipe Out the Jews?

Remember that great song in *Fiddler on the Roof*: *L'Chayim, L'Chayim, to Life*? Christian thought considers life in this world as merely a state preliminary to heaven or hell. Jews see it the other way around. This is the life that counts. Make this one last and make it your best shot. The Jewish cherishing of this life is not hard to understand because, throughout history, rulers of many colors have tried repeatedly to wipe out the Jews.

The word "anti-Semitism" is of recent vintage, but the phenomenon is of long standing. Jews have been accused, sometimes at the same time, of being too rich and too poor, too active and too uninvolved, too powerful and too helpless, too spiritual and too secular, capitalists, and communists. There is definitely something different about just being Jewish. Jews know this. They tend to think that they stick out, even if they don't. Most Jews will seek to be with at least a few other Jews in school, in the neighborhood, on the job – not because Jews are better students, neighbors or co-workers but simply for the comfort of having other Jews around. Ask a Jew who works in a field not populated by many Jews – let's say construction workers or the military – they will tell you that they get by just fine but that, oftentimes, nobody understands them.

Anti-Semitism predates all of today's religions, including Christianity, and is found throughout the world, so it's not a matter of pitting one particular faith or culture against the Jews. Anti-Semitism ebbs and flows. Its common denominator seems to be that those who know Jews the least are the most likely to be anti-Semitic. Today's version in the U.S., where anti-Semitism is making a comeback, consists mostly of desecration of Jewish graves and the defacing of synagogues, although we all were saddened by attacks on Jewish places of worship, such as the synagogue in Pittsburgh. The ever-present problem, of course, is that of ethnic stereotyping. Rabbi Eckstein says: "it's not the Jewish personality, beliefs, actions or social mores, but the fact that he is ...a Jew and, as such, invites their oppression and, in some famous cases, destruction."

Frequently Asked Question No. 7: Has Christianity, and, in Particular, the Catholic Church Been Anti-Semitic?

The conflicts between Christianity and Judaism developed in fits and starts over many centuries. Some Popes protected the Jews, others attacked them. In time of conflict, the main battle cry was always "The Jews Killed Jesus!" As discussed above, this is not historically well supported. In any event, this idea was propagated by the Catholic Church up through the Middle Ages and beyond. Call me cynical, but I think the real reason is that the Jews were the only ones in Europe who, for the most part, wouldn't convert.

In Spain, way back in 589 A.D., Catholicism became the official state religion (which it remains today in many, many countries). The Spanish forbade intermarriage with and segregated the Jews,[3] confiscated their property, put them into ghettos (which today are tourist

---

3 The Jews who migrated from the Middle East to Spain and Portugal became known as the *Sephardim*. Those who moved to the Germanic countries became known as the *Ashkenazim*.

attractions in Andalusia), and, eventually, forced them into either exile or slavery. This continued until the Eighth Century when the Moors took over in Spain and ushered in the Golden Age of Jewish History, during which Jews were treated well and allowed to flourish. This period ended in 1013 when Moslem power was broken and the liberal spirit disintegrated. Nonetheless, please note that Jews and Muslims have not always been in conflict.

The time of the Crusades was, of course, one of the worst periods for Jews. Pope Gregory IX ordered the public burning of the *Talmud* (the Jewish scriptures). Local persecutions began in Western Europe. On their way to Palestine, starting in 1069, the Crusaders killed thousands of Jews wherever they went, particularly if they refused to convert. In fact, it was a teaching of the church that a crusader received salvation by eradicating infidels, leading to the wholesale destruction of hundreds of Jewish communities. In Freiburg, Jews were burned at the stake. In Basel, they were imprisoned. In Strasbourg, 2000 were burned alive in their own cemetery.

In 1215, the Fourth Lateran Council required that Jews wear special badges and live in certain sections of the city. Sound familiar? In the same year, the Catholic Church formalized the doctrine of transubstantiation, which holds that the wine and wafer used in the mass are transformed into the body and blood of Christ. I never did get quite how that works but the anti-Semitic call went out again. Since the Jews killed Jesus once, the argument went, they would try to do it again because they hated this new doctrine. During the next five centuries, thousands of Jews were killed for allegedly breaking into churches and torturing Christ by stealing wafers. I'm not kidding. Google it.

In 1240, four rabbis were delegates to Pope Gregory IX to make nice and "debate" the question of whether the *Talmud* had perverted the teachings of the Bible. Not surprisingly, the rabbis lost the debate and the *Talmud* was burned in the streets of Paris. Massacres and forced conversions were common in Portugal, Spain, France, and Germany.

Jews were expelled from England in 1290, from France in 1394, from Germany in 1350-60, and from Spain in 1492. Even Martin

Luther, the founder of Protestantism which made its appearance at about this time, was profoundly anti-Semitic, infuriated at the Jewish rejection of his new theology. He wrote scathing tracts such as this one:

> If the Jews could kill us all, they would gladly do so, aye, and often do it, especially those who profess to be physicians. They know all that is known about medicine in Germany; they can give poison to a man of which he will die in an hour, or in ten or twenty years.[4]

During the Middle Ages, Jews in Europe were forced to attend church services. The Inquisition in Spain was particularly brutal. Many Jews, exiled from everywhere else, settled in Poland where they became very successful. So, in 1648, the Cossacks attacked the Jews and killed 100,000-300,000 in what is now Poland, Belarus and the Ukraine.

The Age of Enlightenment and the French and American revolutions dramatically improved the Jewish condition in Europe. Jews stepped out into the world more and interacted with Christians without fear of the Pope declaring open season on them. Surprise, surprise, Jews and Christians came to understand and tolerate each other better. This period also marked the alteration of the Jewish faith into a private matter to be practiced in the home and not in the secular world, concurrent with the breakdown of public religion and the separation of church and state. After hundreds of years in Jewish ghettos, integration – for better or for worse – became a realistic goal. The price was some loss of community and shared religious practice, but, for that moment, tolerance of the Jews was high.

Frequently Asked Question No. 8:
What were the *Pogroms* All About?

The condition of Jews in the 19th and early 20th century in Russia,

---

4 Trachtenberg, The Devil and the Jews: The Medieval Conception of the Jew and its Relation to Modern Anti-Semitism (New Haven: Yale University Press, 1943 pp. 97-155)[the quote is on p. 99].

Poland and the other countries of Eastern Europe (most of which were part of the old Soviet Union) was abominable. Jews lived in ghettos, isolated from the surrounding society that didn't want them anyway. In Russia, the Cossacks, on orders from the Tsars, conducted brutal large-scale targeted attacks, called *pogroms* (a Russian word meaning to wreak havoc) wiping out village after village, frequently killing many thousands of Jews. There were pogroms in many eastern countries, hundreds of *pogroms* in all. In some cases, the Jews were wiped out for being Bolsheviks; in other cases, for being anti-Bolshevik. In some, they were reputed to be conspirators against the tsar, in others they were objects because of their "middleman" status, i.e. traders, financiers. Keep in mind that they were middlemen because they could not own property themselves. Many *pogroms* were based on wild and unfounded rumors. In the first 40 years of the twentieth century, 1 ¼ million Jews migrated to the United States.

Frequently Asked Question No. 9:
Have the Jewish People Recovered from the Holocaust?

The Holocaust (or *Shoah*, meaning terrible catastrophe) saw the killing of over six million Jews (about 40% of the total Jewish population in the world). I don't really want to go into the details of the extermination of the Jews and the effect it continues to have today on worldwide Jewish community. The great European libraries of Judaism were destroyed, as were the synagogues, shrines and most Jewish spiritual leaders. If not for the murderous Nazis and their collaborators, estimates are that there would be about 35 million Jews in the world today, as opposed to the actual 10-13 million. Surviving Jews felt their faith challenged. People everywhere lost all optimism about the fate of human kind. The stain of German fascism and the shame of other collaborating states remains very clearly today.

The cry "Never Again" was spawned by Jewish activist organizations vowing that Judaism would suffer no more martyrs. The commitment to Israel increased enormously. Survivors like Elie Wiesel committed themselves to rebuilding the faith and culture.

The post-war period was also one of widespread Christian reflection on attitudes toward Jews. The war had, of course, cast a shadow on Christian-Jewish relations. The inability of gentiles to feel the suffering as the Jews did is a breach that has yet to close. As Elie Wiesel said: "Not all the victims were Jews, but all Jews were victims."

Now, as we get deeper into the 21st Century, after any number of other genocides, we still ask the "Why?" question. Is hatred of the Jews a by-product of other economic and social ills? Is there still a reaction to the *chosen people* claim of the Jews? Is it because Jews are seen as different in ways that other nationalities and religions are not? Is it simply ignorance? All of those questions are rhetorical.

Frequently Asked Question No. 10:
How Good has the United States Been to the Jews?

Again, this requires a step back in time. Please forgive me. I'll make it short. The first Jewish settlers landed in the New World in 1654, arriving in New Amsterdam. They were told, at first, that they would not be admitted. When they finally got in, they were not allowed the basic rights of citizenship: to own land, to trade, hold public office or practice their religion in a public space or in a synagogue. They didn't arrive in chains as so many thousands of African-Americans did, but they didn't exactly get a fine welcome to the land of religious freedom.

The first Jewish congregation was Sephardic, founded in 1740 in Philadelphia. Because the *Sephardim* developed in the mainly Islamic countries of the Middle East, they did not speak Yiddish but rather a mixture of Spanish and Hebrew called *Ladino*. By the time of the Revolutionary War, close to 3000 Jews had trickled into the country.

The first big wave of Jewish immigration came in the 1840's when conditions in Eastern Europe got a lot worse, as discussed above. Many of the new immigrants fanned out to the western and southern regions of the expanding United States. Galveston, Texas had a Jewish mayor in the 1850's. Edna Ferber grew up in Ottumwa, Iowa. By

1880, there were about 250,000 Jews living in America. The next big wave of immigration came around the turn of the century as the *pogroms* raked Jewish villages all over Eastern Europe and America became known to many nationalities as the land of opportunity. Entire villages of poor workers and peasants would emigrate, legally or illegally, whereas the Jews already here, resourceful and well educated, had ascended into the middle classes, just like in *Fiddler on the Roof.*

The Eastern European Jews arrived mainly at Ellis Island and settled on the lower east side of New York. There, they knew the poverty of the immigrant classes, working in the sweatshops of New York and facing the constant battle between assimilation and the preservation of their culture and religion.

Immigration dropped off after this second wave until refugees were allowed admittance before and after World War II. During the war itself, the U.S. government was tragically slow to admit refugees from the Holocaust (see the WWII political timeline).

After the war, many Jews, for fear of being identified as Jews or just to change a complicated Slavic-sounding name to a smooth American one, changed the family name and tried to assimilate into the larger society to spare their children from the same horror. Of the 13 million Jews in the world today, the large majority lives either in the U.S. or Israel.

CHRONOLOGY OF THE U.S. GOVERNMENT RESPONSE TO THE HOLOCAUST

1938 July   President Roosevelt convenes the Evian conference where only one of the 33 countries convened agrees to accept Jewish refugees from Germany [the Dominican Republic]

1938 November Kristallnacht, or The Night of Broken Glass, in Germany, results in the destruction of hundreds of synagogues, Jewish businesses, homes, hospitals and schools, as well as the arrest of 30,000 Jewish men who were sent to concentration camps in Germany.

1939 February   The Wagner-Rogers bill to admit 20,000 Jewish refugees into the U.S. dies in committee

1939 June   The refugee ship *S.S. St. Louis,* with over 900 Jewish refugees from Hamburg aboard is refused permission to dock at a number of U.S. and Canadian ports. The ship and its passengers eventually return to Hamburg in northern Germany and many of the passengers died in concentration camps

S.S. St. Louis

1941 July	Yiddish daily newspapers in New York City report the massacres of thousands of Jews by the Nazis invading Russia
1941 October	The New York Times reports thousands of Jews massacred in Galicia
1942 October	On October 8, the U.S. consulate in Geneva is informed of a plan to murder all the Jews in Europe. The information is passed to the U.S. State Department three days later.
1942 October	A bill in the U.S. House to open the doors to refugees from France dies in committee.
1943 January	The U.S. State Department receives information that 6,000 Jews a day are being killed in one location in Poland. The Department asks its legation in Switzerland to stop sending reports of mass murder to private citizens.
1943 April	British and U.S. officials hold a two-week conference in Bermuda on ways to rescue European Jewish refugees. Nothing comes of it.
1943 June	U.S. admits that its consulates in Spain are withholding visas for refugees who had already been approved.
1943 July	Polish resistance fighter Jan Karski holds his famous meeting with President Roosevelt to give his eyewitness account of the death camps, the first Roosevelt had heard. He pleads for action, including the bombing of the extermination camps in Poland. Roosevelt refuses.

1943 September	A House bill to temporarily admit refugees "who don't endanger public safety" fails to reach the House floor.
1943 October	Roosevelt refuses to meet with 400 Orthodox rabbis gathered outside the White House with petitions calling for the establishment of a rescue agency.
1944 January	Roosevelt establishes the War Refugee Board which opened its first refugee camp in North Africa in May.
1944 June	Five days before the D-Day invasion in Normandy, Roosevelt agrees to allow 1,000 mostly Jewish refugees in Italy to come to a camp in the U.S. An appeal later in the month by the Jewish underground in Slovakia to bomb the deportation routes to Auschwitz is turned down by the War Department.
1944 August	The War Department writes that bombing Auschwitz would divert air power from "decisive operations elsewhere" even though, six days later and, again, on September 13, U.S. bombers destroyed the factory areas of Auschwitz, less then five miles from the gas chambers.
1945 January	Death marches of Jews to the interior of Germany begin. 250,000 die. The State Department announces that those guilty of war crimes will be punished.

Frequently Asked Question No. 11: What is the Difference Between Judaism and Zionism?

Once again wading into deep waters without a paddle, I'll start by saying that Zionism is not a religious belief. It's a political belief. Its credo is that the Jews have a special right to the land previously known as Palestine. Not all Jews are Zionists. Not by any means, since Zionism emerged late in the 19th Century but didn't really take hold until after the War. Most Jews, however, support Israel as a nation-state in one way or another.

A little background: Nachmanides and other Jewish prophets said that to live outside Israel is a violation of Jewish law. Arabs say that Israel is a creation of the war of 1947-1949 and that, for almost 2,000 years before that, the land of Palestine has been rightfully the state of the Palestinian people. Starting in the 19th Century, Zionist Jewish writers began addressing the need to resettle Palestine. We are tired, they wrote, of living as strangers in many countries for thousands of years, unable to integrate without abandoning Jewish life, and feeling that anti-Semitism is an incurable gentile disease. In 1896, Theodor Herzl wrote The Jewish State which became a manifesto for Zionists looking for a homeland.

How did this happen? In 1917, the British, in the Balfour Declaration, approved of the use of Palestine (which the Brits had conveniently just plucked from Turkey) as a homeland for the Jewish people. The waves of emigration started, particularly from Eastern Europe where the *pogroms* had gone from bad to unspeakably worse. Palestinians and Arab nationalists were understandably upset and voiced their dissent leading to a revocation of the Balfour Declaration in 1939 and imposing a limit on Jewish emigration – just when Jews needed Palestine most to flee from Hitler. Even after World War II and the Holocaust, Britain still refused to lift the limits and no country welcomed the surviving Jews with open arms. The Zionists persisted and the British turned the problem over to the newly created United Nations which carved up Palestine and, on May 14, 1948, declared Israel an independent nation. The next day, a coalition of Arab armies rose up and ten months of fighting ensued. Israel basically won that war and 700,000 Palestinians became refugees from their homes and the country was partitioned into Israel and the occupied territory of Palestine, which includes the West Bank and Gaza.

Then there was the war of 1967 during which the Israelis conquered more Palestinian land, turning it into the "occupied territories," separated from Israel by the infamous wall. Since that war, what remains of Palestine has been reduced by a large number of Israeli settlements that the Palestinians and most governments of the world see as illegal. The conflict that persists today has Israelis on one side who feel that the Palestinians and their Arab allies are a threat to the existence of Israel and, on the other side, the Palestinian people feel that their homeland was partitioned out of existence by the U.N. and that the Israelis are occupiers. Today, the word Zionism refers not just to support for Israel but also to support for what is perceived to be aggressive Israeli policies toward the Arabs. Most Jews support the State of Israel (of which they are automatic citizens). Not all Jews support Zionism.

CHAPTER 3

HOW TO GO TO TEMPLE WITHOUT LOOKING LIKE AN IDIOT: THE JEWISH RELIGION

IT TOOK ME years to understand that Judaism is more than a religion or an ethnicity. It's a way of life. Even if a Jew is an atheist, they are still ethnically Jewish. But Jewish is also more than an ethnicity. Christians are usually either Catholic or Protestant in addition to their nationality. I'm Italian-American with a Catholic upbringing. There are three major sects of Islam (some say four) but a Muslim is also from the country of their ancestors. A Jew may come from Russia or Germany or Poland but the primary identity is as a Jew – first and foremost.

You will often hear a Jewish person say: "I'm not a practicing Jew." That doesn't mean they aren't Jewish or even that they have rejected Judaism. To be a practicing Jew does not only mean to go to temple and observe Jewish religious laws. It also means that you live your life as a Jewish person. It's more than the sum of its parts. Even if a Jewish person chooses to be a non-practicing Jew, it's very rare to find a Jew who will completely separate from being Jewish. Not even Jews for Jesus. One can ignore Italian ancestral roots. I personally know Italian-Americans who do not talk with their hands, sing, or eat pasta several times a week. Change the last name and you're just another Mediterranean type. Anybody can reject their Christian religion – and I mean really reject it. And it's gone. But to say you're no longer Jewish – just doesn't happen. Anybody can learn not to say *Oy!* and to have no sense of humor and to work very hard on avoiding any stereotypical behavior you can imagine but that person is still, at the core, Jewish.

This is very hard to explain. Jews reading this may say: "This guy doesn't get it," and, to some extent, I agree. The religion and the culture are totally intertwined in a way that Christians do not experience. In Judaism, the Sabbath and the religious holidays are of great importance but just as important are the habits, values and customs of being Jewish. A gentile in a Jewish world will eventually be exposed to all of them.

The Frequently Asked Questions

IS A GENTILE WELCOME AT A SYNAGOGUE SERVICE?

There is absolutely no reason to be uptight about being a gentile at a Jewish religious service. First, you are welcome. There is no religious prohibition against a gentile attending a service. You may have to purchase a ticket in advance for the High Holidays (higher prices sometimes for non-members) but, even in those congregations, I've never heard of anyone being turned away. And, of course, in these days of high security and safety precautions, a reservation may be necessary at some services and those reservations may be restricted to members. Susan and I recently went to Yom Kippur services at a synagogue in Berlin that, otherwise, is quite secure. Of course, we asked for advance clearance but, even then, it turned out not to be necessary.

CAN I BE A MEMBER OF THE CONGREGATION WITHOUT BEING JEWISH?

Until recently, only Reform and Reconstructionist Jewish congregations would allow a gentile to be an actual card-carrying member of the synagogue. In non-Reform congregations, the family membership would ordinarily be held in the name of the Jewish spouse. Recently, however, in the face of declining membership and increasing inter-marriage, many Conservative congregations give full membership to the non-Jewish spouse. I will explain these distinctions later.

WHAT TO WEAR?

To be on the safe side, dress nicely, even in hot weather. At informal services, such as children's services, you'll see informal dress though I have never seen jeans, shorts, halter tops or even bare arms on a grown-up. In fact, I learned my lesson the hard way many years ago when, at an evening *Kol Nidre* service at the end of the High Holidays, I was the only male not wearing a coat and tie. There is no need to get *fatootsed* for ordinary services.

If you're a male and going to *shul* for a religious service, the first thing you decide when you get there is whether or not to wear the skull cap which is called a *yarmulke* or *kippah*. Many synagogues have a box of them near the chapel entrance for the congregation. If it's a Reform temple, it's not mandatory that men wear the *yarmulke*, although the Jewish men usually do. It's pretty much your own choice. If you're not Jewish, it's fine to wear the *yarmulke* as a sign of respect. I always do. In a Conservative or Orthodox temple, it's ordinarily a requirement. In all likelihood, an usher will hand you one if you forget. In fact, the Orthodox male will keep his head covered at all times in public even though there is no mandate under Jewish law for the wearing of a head-covering at all. It's merely a continuation of the historical custom. Not to mention that it's a mark of distinction from gentile men who do not wear head-coverings in church. In any event, the only guys who look better in a *yarmulke* are bald guys like me.

Only married Orthodox women wear hats or wigs as an observance of the Biblical teaching that chaste and modest women keep their heads covered. The unmarried Orthodox do not cover their heads so that men will immediately know their marital status. In

Conservative and Reform congregations, women will typically wear something on their heads but it's discretionary.

The *talis* (sometimes written *tallit*) is the fringed scarf that Jewish men wear at morning services in temple. The Orthodox have a specially made *talis* that they wear all the time under their clothes. At synagogue, the men will gather up the fringes and kiss them when praying. It reminds them of the community of Judaism. When the Ark is carried around, the men will touch it with the *talis*. It's inappropriate for a non-Jew to wear the *talis*. Don't worry about it. They don't pass them out at the door.

WHERE DO I SIT?

In a reform temple, sit anyplace that is not reserved. When you walk into a Conservative temple, it's hard to notice but people usually sit in the same seats, week after week. That's probably because they paid for those particular seats in their temple dues. Like season tickets. Conservative Jewish children often sit in the same seats at *shul* for their whole childhood and, as adults, they may very well inherit the same seats from their parents. Sometimes, life-long friendships start with the temple seating arrangements. If you're in a synagogue like that, you're probably a guest of someone and should sit in his or her seats. If you're not a guest, sit in the back. If you make a mistake and sit in somebody's seat, no big deal. It's a dying custom anyway. Many more modern congregations don't have their own temples, so where you sit is not a problem.

WHAT IF I'M AT AN ORTHODOX SERVICE?

First of all, going to an Orthodox service means you're in for the long haul. Much longer than the services of other Jewish denominations. When you enter an Orthodox temple, you will notice right away the men and the women are segregated. The men will be downstairs and the women upstairs or on the other side of the center aisle. The women may also have a separate entrance. There are two reasons for this: 1) at services, you're supposed to keep your mind on prayer, and 2) women are not required by Jewish law to attend *shul*, therefore they are not expected to take a major role in the service or in the life of the synagogue. Truth be known, the *Talmud* says a lot of things about women that are dissonant with the modern era: woman's primary duties are as wife and mother; they are to be discouraged from higher education or religious studies; they are to play a limited role in synagogue life. Obviously, only the most traditional Jews observe these teachings. In any event, I'm told the air-conditioning sometimes doesn't work as well upstairs and the sight lines aren't always the best so it's common to hear the women chatting about other things during the service.

Many temples will have ushers who will point out available seats and keep you from entering when the Ark is open.

DO I JOIN IN THE PRAYERS?

In Reform congregations (and, face it, that's where most gentiles wind up), there is no problem with participating in the prayers. Many prayers are in English or are transliterated so you can try your sight-reading skills. Conservative and Orthodox, however, have traditionally thought that active participation in the service by a non-Jew is of no religious significance and is inappropriate. This, too, is changing. Most Jews don't see this as an issue and so they don't take it all that seriously. If it isn't done exactly right, we'll get it right one of these times. I have been complimented on my Hebrew pronunciation of prayers. Jews expect less of us.

There are usually two books to deal with at each service: the prayer book and the Old Testament. Readings will switch back and forth between the two, with the rabbi usually announcing the page. The books are usually in both Hebrew and English. The cantor, with or without the congregation joining in, sings many of the prayers. Usually, the singing is of the preceding or succeeding prayer and it's almost always in Hebrew, so it makes it hard for most gentiles to join in.

Remember, the books open from the back and go toward the front.

WHAT ARE SOME THINGS TO NOTICE
ABOUT THE INTERIOR OF THE TEMPLE?

One of the first things you'll notice when you walk into any Jewish temple: no God. No Holy Trinity, no statues, no paintings of Biblical scenes, no frescoes, no crucifixions, no angels and no resurrections. In fact, you will not see any visual representations of any Jewish idol. There's a good reason for that: there are no Jewish idols. As to God, the reason is very simple. Jews do not believe that you can really conceptualize God in any corporeal sense and they don't believe, obviously, in Jesus Christ or the Holy Trinity. Not only can you not ascribe features to God, i.e. male, white, long hair, skinny, etc. but you can't even give God a human form. This is because Jews believe that the essence of God is beyond human comprehension.

As to idols such as the Virgin Mary, the Apostles and saints, there are none of those either. Judaism doesn't have any. Aside from putting a tremendous cramp in the religious artifacts business, the effect of it is that Jews don't really understand sainthood, just like they don't get the angels, the apostles, or the subject matter of almost any

Renaissance painting or Italian opera. For those of Catholic background, try explaining the mysteries of the rosary to a Jew sometime and see how much you really understand about your own religion. Then, try to explain the process of canonization and sainthood, with the grounds for waiver of the five-year rule, and the certification of miracles, including the posthumous ones. It's kind of like explaining the Electoral College.

I digress. Back to the temple. Before you in the main chapel or sanctuary, usually facing east, is what you might take to be an altar. A raised platform, a velvet or silk curtain or wood panel in the middle which is obviously hiding something, a podium in the center or one on each side, various prayers or sayings in Hebrew on the wall, perhaps a nice stained glass. The podium is called the *bima*. The *Torah* is read from here. In reform synagogues, at least, you may see a choir loft with an organ. That should make you feel more comfortable. Much of the Jewish service is sung. Male choirs are common in Orthodox synagogues. Much of the singing is participatory, so be prepared to test out the vocal cords.

SO WHAT'S BEHIND THE CURTAIN?

The *Torah* is scrolled up inside the Holy Ark which, behind the curtain or panel, looks like a closed cabinet. The Ark contains the most sacred objects and is the focal point of the synagogue. It is normally placed against the eastern wall of the synagogue so that worshippers will be facing Jerusalem. The original Ark was in the tabernacle that the children of Israel carried with them during their 40-year trek in the desert.

In the Ark are two tablets on which are inscribed the Ten Commandments. Also in the Ark are several *Toro* (plural of *Torah*) written on parchment and scrolled up in the Ark. At all religious services, there will be readings from the *Torah*. The *Torah* is the first five books of the Bible (what Christians would call the Old Testament): Genesis, Exodus, Leviticus, Numbers, and Deuteronomy. The New Testament is not part of Jewish scripture. The *Torah* is divided into

54 sections so that you can basically get through the whole book every year.

WHAT'S THE DIFFERENCE BETWEEN THE LEADER ON THE LEFT AND THE ONE ON THE RIGHT?

The person on the right is the rabbi. The leader of Jewish religious life is the rabbi. He or she teaches and interprets the *Torah* and the *Talmud* (which contains the writings of the Jewish prophets). In modern life, the rabbi has also become like a priest or a minister in that he or she not only conducts the service but also tends to the congregation by visiting the sick, counseling members of the temple, etc. Traditionally, rabbis were not ordained and did not lead services. Today, most rabbis are trained in Jewish seminaries called *yeshivas*. The first woman rabbi was ordained in 1978 in, of all places, Monmouth, New Jersey. Though the numbers of female rabbis are still small, all progressive Jews (that means non-Orthodox) recognize women rabbis. The rabbi will lead the service. A good rabbi will keep the service participatory.

In terms of vestments you will see, the rabbi doesn't even get to wear the colorful and symbolic robes that the priest and some ministers wear. Usually, a rabbi wears what the congregants wear – for males, the *yarmulke*, maybe the *talis*. If Orthodox, add maybe the black hat, black suit and long beard. For females, there is no *de rigeur* outfit.

The second most noticeable member of the cast is the cantor – the person at the podium on the left. Formerly, the cantor was any member of the congregation who had a good voice and could sing parts of the service in temple. Now, the cantor is most often a paid musician who not only sings well (and perhaps plays an instrument) but also has degrees or training in Jewish history, religion and law. He or she will sing at Sabbath services, the holidays, *bar* and *bat mitzvahs* and other feasts. The cantor is also the person who will teach the kids to sing in Sunday school and to teach the *bar* and *bar mitzvah* kids how to sing the *Haftorah* portion they will sing at the ceremony (more later).

If another person is up there for the whole service, it's usually the President of the congregation or other lay leaders. They are the people who make the announcements and generally help out with everything going on up on the *bima* – think stage manager.

IS THE SYNAGOGUE BUILDING
USED FOR ANYTHING BESIDES SERVICES?

The synagogue is as much an all-purpose building as any church that has the youth group and the Bible study group and the ladies auxiliary meeting in the basement (do they still have those?). Traditionally, the synagogue is not only a house of prayer but also of assembly and study. It's a real center of Jewish life, kind of like a second home, from the study groups to the teen groups, choir practice, and the rabbi's storytelling hour. Our former temple had a shelter for the homeless every Wednesday night until the pandemic.

Sunday school or Hebrew school for the kids is easily one of the most important functions of the synagogue. There are not that many everyday, all-day Jewish schools. The large majority of modern Jews send their children to public or non-sectarian private schools (although we know one young Jewish man who went to Catholic high school and can recite his Catholic prayers as well as anyone). Typically, Hebrew school is four days a week after secular school. Sunday is another more elaborate operation. A child who is to be *bar* or *bat mitzvahed* will embark on a serious course of study at 10 or 11 years old, including regular sessions with the cantor and the lay teachers. Otherwise, Hebrew school helps out those parents who feel the need to offer their children at least a taste of Jewish education. I have one son who went to temple events to meet girls and another son who, despite his frequent Sunday morning protests, enjoyed learning about culture and religion and has come to identify himself as Jewish (no, I don't mind).

One big difference is that the synagogue is not used for either weddings or funerals. We'll talk about that in the ceremony section.

WHY DON'T SYNAGOGUES LOOK A LITTLE MORE LIKE CHURCHES?

In the United States, most synagogues are relatively plain, modern-looking buildings – not at all ornate like cathedrals or even your average Protestant church. No spires, no bells, no neo-Baroque architecture. The Star of David or the *menorah* are common design elements. In metropolitan areas, most temples are in the suburbs because of the exodus of most Jews from the cities during the 20th Century. A city *shul* will probably look a little more architecturally distinctive. There may be a main chapel and a couple of side, smaller chapels. There should also be a large number of windows in the main sanctuary. Ideally there are twelve windows, representing the tribes of Israel. The overall effect is that the main room is usually large, airy, and naturally well lighted.

There are obvious exceptions to the common look. The country's first synagogue, in Newport, Rhode Island, is a gorgeous wooden building that fits right in with the colonial look of the city. It was built in the 18th century and continues today as an Orthodox temple. The country's first reform synagogue was built in Charleston, South Carolina, also in the 18th century where it stands today as a place of worship and tourist attraction because of its lovely period architecture and unique artifacts.

WHAT DO YOU DO WITH THE KIDS DURING THE SERVICES?

Children of all ages are welcome at services. Many synagogues provide child-care during service for the younger kids. Some have a special service downstairs for the kids. When that service is over, the children join the parents upstairs. The children who attend the service are generally well behaved but they are not constantly shushed. So you'll hear them talking or even playing, and they all go to the bathroom every ten minutes. In my experience in church, whenever a kid made any noise that could be heard, a parent would immediately rush them out of the service. In synagogue, the kids may also come and go but it's much more laid-back.

WHAT HAPPENS AT THE SERVICE?

It depends on what service you are attending. In Catholicism, there used to be a High Mass and Low Mass and they were structurally pretty much the same, no matter what church you were in. One was longer. The weekly gospel, the epistle and maybe the sermon are all that change. In most Protestant denominations, there is more variation. This is more like Judaism. It depends on the week of the year, the religious rite or festival. It will be different every week. One of my gentile friends thinks that the temple service is "disorganized." He was disoriented, as a practicing Catholic, when he couldn't see the structure of the service and couldn't tell where each part was in relation to other parts. " The rabbi says a prayer, then some other people come up and pray, then you sing a song, then the rabbi says another prayer and ad-libs for awhile, then everybody prays again – I needed a road map." Spoken like a true Catholic where the Gloria always follows the Credo.

In fact, there is a basic structure to the service. A preliminary issue: you need at least ten Jewish adults to even have the service. Traditionally, the adults constituting this *minyan* were counted only if male. That has since changed, except with the Orthodox. The service begins with a welcome or "warm-up" prayer. Then, there is a call to prayers, two blessings, a statement of faith in God, including a reading from the *Torah*, two more blessings, a prayer which is focused on the particular week, a *kaddish* (which is a concluding prayer for those who have died) and a concluding hymn. The key blessings are called the *Amidah*, recited while standing, and usually including 13 requests of God. Each of these parts has a liturgical name, meaning, and history that you can find at any number of Jewish websites. Frequently during the service, there are songs and responsive readings. Some are in Hebrew (the percentage depends on what kind of synagogue you are in), others are in English. I have always joined in the responsive readings in English. In fact, after all these years, there are a few that I can repeat in Hebrew. I think the participation of everyone is welcome and that for a gentile to join in the readings is really only a sign of respect.

As to who leads these prayers or *aliyahs*, that depends. It depends on what the congregation has decided for which type of service: Sabbath, holidays, bar/bat mitzvahs and the like. To lead an *aliyah* is an honor and it is usually reserved for congregation leaders or those who have made special contributions. All of this can be crammed into a 45-minute Reform service or a three-hour Orthodox service.

Some of the readings will be from the *haftarah* which is the Book of Prophets. At a *Bar* or *Bat Mitzvah*, there are readings from the Prophets or the *Torah* by several people, including a section read by the kid being *Bar* or *Bat Mitzvahed*. This will be their first *aliyah*. Each person leading a prayer is called up to the *bima* for the reading and, afterward, each will shake hands with the others who are sitting on the *bima*. On the High Holidays (*Rosh Hashanah* and *Yom Kippur*), a *shofar*, or ram's horn, will be sounded to remind people of times of war or *pogrom* when the horn was used to sound the alarm. It's sort of like a bugle but it makes a God-awful sound and is apparently very hard to blow.

Don't be surprised if more male Jews participate in the Hebrew readings than the females. More males were *bar mitzvahed* than females were *bat mitzvahed* and that's when you learn these prayers

Whether a gentile can lead a prayer is a matter for the congregation or the rabbi to decide. Reconstructionists and Reform generally seem to believe that one can join the Jewish people in prayer without subscribing to the religion. But can a gentile be counted to form the 10-person *minyan*? Can a gentile be called to the *Torah*? Can a gentile be on the synagogue's Board or Chair a committee, or even be President? These are harder questions. To some, allowing gentiles full participation is a way of opening Judaism to other religious traditions. To others, it is a threat to the integrity of the Jewish religion. If you're at that point, you don't need this book anymore.

WHAT'S THE MOST COMMON JEWISH PRAYER?

Most Jewish prayers seem to start with the following line which, if pronounced anywhere near correctly, is not only a sign of respect for the religion but also very impressive that a gentile would know to speak these words in Hebrew. *Baruch ata adonoy, eloheinu melech ha-olom*. OK, you try it. Bah-ROOK-ah-TAW-ah-doh-NOY-el-o-HAY-noo-MEL-ek-haw-aw-LOM. It means, "Blessed art Thou, O Lord our God, King of the Universe." Then the Hebrew continues in different directions depending on whether it's Sabbath, or Hannukah, Passover, etc. At the end of every prayer, you *Amen* (but pronounced "aw-mayn)."

WHAT ELSE DO I NEED TO KNOW ABOUT THE SERVICE?

Unlike church, no collection basket is passed. Most congregations require members to pay yearly dues. You will also notice that, like church, there is a lot of stand up and sit down. The rabbi will tell everybody what to do. The good news is there's no kneeling or genuflecting at a Jewish service. No pressure on the knees. With a couple of unusual exceptions, it's fine to walk in or out of a service. Depending on the synagogue, you may also notice that a lot of people talk to each other during the service. After all, the synagogue is supposed to be a Jew's second home. I always found that strange given that no socializing was allowed during Mass in the Catholic Church. People in temple will sometimes just take a break from the service and start talking to a neighbor or go out for a minute. The rabbi may not like it, but it happens.

You will also notice that, at any point during prayers, some members of the congregation (usually men in my experience) will stand and rock back and forth, bending forward from the waist. This is called *davening*. They're just praying. They may also be mumbling the prayers out loud in Hebrew. In synagogue, you can pray whenever you want, no matter what everybody else seems to be doing. Maybe you were late and you're just catching up.

WHAT DO JEWS MEAN WHEN THEY SAY THEY ARE CELEBRATING THE SABBATH?

Shabbat is the Sabbath and it starts at sundown on Friday night. To a practicing Jew, observing *Shabbat* is the most important of the precepts in the *Torah*. It represents the climax of the week of creation and signals that we are to rest on the seventh day. Sound familiar? But, for Jews, the seventh day is Saturday. More than that, *Shabbat* is a time to put the world aside and "get clean." It's a time to be proud and to restore oneself.

Shabbat is also a very family and home-oriented event. Many Jews light candles at home and a have a Friday night, post-sunset family meal. They may say a prayer (*Kiddush*) about creation or the emancipation from slavery over cups of wine. Traditional Jews will also refrain from business or mundane activities from the *Shabbat* dinner until sunset Saturday. They will also refrain from working, writing, cooking, carrying, sewing, tearing, cutting – anything that can be seen as work. Food, usually stews, is prepared in advance by the observant. When you think about it, observing the Sabbath as an

Orthodox Jew can make your life very difficult for a day. Imagine tearing the toilet paper in advance to avoid tearing on *shabbes* or turning out the refrigerator light every Friday so that it doesn't go on when you open the door and setting all the lights and appliances on timers so that you don't flick switches. There are 39 categories of work that are prohibited because it alters the environment. Each relates back to a specific portion of the *Torah*. To be sure, only the Orthodox or particularly literal Jews will observe the Sabbath to this point.

If a *shabbes* service is the one you're attending, it will convene after the Friday meal or Saturday morning. Everybody says "good *shabbes*" to each other as a greeting. The rest of the day, at least for the observant, is seen as a special time for family togetherness without TV, cellphones, computers or even telephones.

TEN THINGS **NOT** TO DO WHILE IN TEMPLE

1. Genuflect when passing before the Ark.

2. Make a sign of the cross at any time.

3. Stand up every time you hear a bell ring.

4. Put money in any basket.

5. Eat, drink or conduct business.

6. Touch the *Torah* when it is carried by your seat.

7. Take pictures or videos or talk on your cell phone

8. Make any comments about how so many of the people don't look Jewish.

9. Ask a person whose head is bobbing up and down if he needs help.

10. "Shush" little children or anybody else.

WHAT ARE THE BASIC RELIGIOUS DIFFERENCES BETWEEN CHRISTIANITY AND JUDAISM

This part of the chapter is short for two reasons: the Jewish religion doesn't have as many rules, regulations and icons as Christianity does and, secondly, a large percentage of American Jews don't really practice the religion anyway. This is not to demean their Jewishness. It just means that many Jews don't go to temple and are somewhat less interested generally in the religious aspects of Judaism. We also need to recognize that, with increasing inter-marriage between Jews and gentiles, religion sometimes takes a back seat. Author Philip Weiss put it best in this excerpt:

> As I soon learned when I began looking into Jewish identity, I'm what sociologists call an ethnic. My sense of myself as Jewish draws on tribal traits, values, culture, language. My parents were the children of immigrants and kept American culture and values as far outside the house as they were able. Not that they were religious. My father is a scientist and disdainful of religious belief. Still, my family joined a conservative congregation in the sixties, as many other Jewish families did, becaue of the "black mail of bar miztvah (referring to the practice of not conducting *bar/bat mitzvahs* at the temple unless the family was a dues-paying member)."

IN THE BEGINNING...

Jews do Adam and Eve but they don't do original sin. Original sin is, to Catholics and some Protestants, the ultimate guilt trip. No matter how good you are or how many times you repent, you can never completely wipe away the stain of the forbidden fruit. The theological basis of Christian guilt is thus easily explained. Jewish guilt comes from letting your mother sit home alone by the phone. Jews believe that God created the world but the specific details of the creation process are not central to Jewish thought.

SO WHAT'S A SIN?

In Judaism, there is no real concept of sin. No mortal sins, no venial sins, no acts of contrition, no penance and no confessional. To Jews, nobody's perfect. The *Talmud* teaches that you see your mistakes, you admit them, and you try again. That's the spirit of the Christian confession as well but, in Judaism, there's no confession to another person behind a black curtain and no embarrassed recitation of the unspeakably sinful things you've done.

It's a sin if a Jew does not live up to his or her potential in this life (I think you get to make the call yourself). Jews don't have the laundry list of sins and punishments. While a Christian may be concerned with saving the soul, the key question for Jews is between good and evil on this earth. There is no purgatory where you work off your sins. It's all about this material world.

Jews don't do the virgin birth, the Trinity, the Pope, or any number of ground-level Christian concepts. They don't believe in the miracles in the Bible. They don't have the dogma that Christianity has developed around the Ten Commandments. They also don't have the dogma about human nature or freedom of choice. They're just not into dogma.

DO JEWS BELIEVE IN THE TEN COMMANDMENTS?

Yes, in fact, they do. Jews actually claim ownership since it was Moses who came down from the mountaintop with the two tablets. The Jewish and Christian versions are only slightly different.

WHAT'S THE REQUIRED READING?

There is no official book that contains all the teachings of Judaism. Gentiles have the Old and New Testament of the Bible. Jews recognize the Old Testament as well. But, for Jews, it's the *Torah* which is the basic source of Jewish law and tradition. The *Torah* is the first five books of the Old Testament (which gives the two religions a common meeting ground) but, it must be said, many of the Old Testament's teachings have been reinterpreted out of Jewish existence. In addition, there are the teachings of the Prophets that are used to explain the Old Testament but there is no New Testament Bible (which, in reality, just explains the Old Testament). Then, and probably most importantly, to study Judaism as a religion is to study the *Talmud*. The *Talmud*, all 63 books of it, is a thousand years of commentary (preceded by "oral tradition") on the Bible or *Torah* and on the teachings of the Prophets who were the "scholars" of incipient Judaism and interpreters of the *Torah*. The *Talmud* says that there were 48 Prophets and 7 Prophetesses, including the first two prophets, Moses and Abraham. You can dedicate your life to studying the *Talmud*, just as some Christians are totally dedicated to the Old and New Testament. The difference is that even most Orthodox Jews believe that the meaning of the *Torah* evolves and there is no static interpretation that must be literally obeyed. That's why every non-Orthodox rabbi is seen as having the authority to interpret the *Torah* in his or her own way. After all, they are the sons and daughters of the Prophets. And, remember, there is no Pope to hand down the definitive rules.

Let me give you an example. When electricity was invented, many rabbis got together to decide whether electricity violated the edict of the *Torah* "Thou shall not burn fire in all your dwelling on the Sabbath day." The majority decided that electricity operated on the same principles as fire and was therefore not to be turned on and off on *Shabbat*. Orthodox Jews observe this interpretation today. Conservative Jews believe that today's rabbis are, as mentioned, the sons and daughters of the Prophets and therefore the interpretation of the *Torah* can evolve if the Jewish community can no longer accept a particular *Talmudic* interpretation of the *Torah*. The Reform Jew, after studying the *Torah* and the *Talmud*, is free, as an individual, to accept or reject the *Talmud*'s interpretation. The *Talmud*, to the Reform Jew, is not infallible.

The *haftorah*, on the other hand is the Jewish gospel. These are the writings of the Prophets. There is a special *haftorah* reading for each *Shabbes* service. Since many *Shabbes* services include a *bar* or *bat mitzvah*, you may well hear a 13-year old reciting the *haftorah* for that day. Or maybe singing it in the cracking and off-pitch 13-year old voice.

About the only two things that all Jews will agree on is their shared history and the belief that Jesus Christ was neither divine nor the savior. You might ask why, with so much of the Old Testament in common, did the Jews make Jesus Christ the deal-breaker? Remember that Judaism is much older than Christianity and, in Judaism, there was no official belief on the nature of God, the universe, or the meaning of life. God, to religious Jews, has always been ever-present but not in the human form that Christianity gives to him (or her). God, to Jews, did not come down from heaven but rather is a great teacher of morality here on earth. Unitarian Protestants also believe God to be like a Prophet and not particularly divine. There is that in common.

The idea of God, to Jews, is much more personal and intimate. There's very little of that awe-inspiring omnipotence or omniscience that I, for one, was taught in Catholic school. To be fair, modern Christianity teaches that God, albeit a cosmic force, is embodied in many moral values, such as justice or mercy. This notion is more consistent with Jewish belief.

There's so much room for personal opinion in Judaism but, make no mistake, Judaism is much more concerned with actions than beliefs. The Messiah is coming, however, and it is the conduct of mankind that will determine when that happens: some say it will happen when the world is most sinful and needy; others say it's when the world is deserving. But when it happens, the doctrine goes, all people will get along, the temple in Jerusalem will be rebuilt, and there will be no hatred, intolerance or war. Looks like it might be awhile.

There is some controversy about the notion of an after-life. Jewish scholars have downplayed it over the last 200 or so years. Recently, however, there has been a resurgence of belief in immortality and a rediscovery of Biblical passages to support that idea. A couple of things are clear: first, there is no hell as we imagine it. No devil or Satan, no eternal fires. Second, if there is a heaven, it's not a gated community where you live in opulence and in the company of everybody you knew who went before you. In Judaism, there is not one popular conception so the goal is to live this life in the here and now.

WHAT ARE THE DIFFERENT KINDS OF JUDAISM?

Without getting too technical, there are four main strains to modern American Judaism: Orthodox, Conservative, Reform and then the "progressive" wing, the largest of which is the Reconstructing Judaism movement. Judaism also includes many congregations of their own religious orientation but not subscribing to any particular tendency within Judaism. I'm not counting all the sub-branches, like the Hasidic, Lubavitch, Haredim, or any of the sects popular mostly in Israel, like the Sephardim, Ashkenazic and Misrahi. If you're from or familiar with New York City, you know the Williamsburg community in Brooklyn, which is home to the ultra-orthodox Jews who wear the black hats, long black robes, beards, women with wigs and the long, perfectly curled braid of hair hanging around the ears of Hasidic men. You're not getting invited to their synagogues anyway.

Most of the modern strains appeared in opposition to Orthodox Judaism in 19th Century Germany, when many Jews wanted to get rid of most of the bothersome Jewish laws but retain the basics and the spirit of Judaism. Reform Jews, for example, are seen by Orthodox Jews a lot like Unitarians are viewed by other Protestants. Atheists, infidels. The Orthodox think the Reform have discarded the core Jewish value. The ultra-Orthodox think that Reform Jews are actually a threat to Judaism. Some have urged that intermarriages and conversions not be recognized and that the Orthodox should not even associate with the non-Orthodox. Happens in every family or, in this case, tribe. The proof is in the pudding, however, as intermarriage continues to grow as does Reform Jewry.

So, what's the difference? The Orthodox see the *Torah* and the

Talmud as absolute and immutable. To them, the 613 teachings in the *Torah,* as elaborated upon by the Prophets, are binding on all Jews. There are almost 1500 Orthodox synagogues in the U.S. with close to 2 million members and growing, if only because the Orthodox typically have large families. According to a Pew Research Center survey in 2015, 14% of all Jews identify as Orthodox.

The Conservative movement was organized in 1913. Conservatives recognize the binding nature of Jewish law but believe that the law evolves and adapts. It's the centrist position on Jewish religious custom between the Orthodox and Reform. The same Pew survey concluded that about 22% of all American Jews self-identify as Conservative.

The Reform movement was the first breakaway from Orthodox Judaism in the 19th Century: 1819 in Germany and 1846 in the United States. Reform Jews see the laws of the *Torah* and *Talmud* as guidelines to be adopted or rejected. So, only those customs and practices which the denomination has chosen to observe are observed. The choice will be an individual matter, not one dictated by the congregation or some religious doctrine. The Reform movement concentrates on those ethical and universal ideals consistent with basic Jewish tenets. Reform Jews don't usually "keep kosher (more on that later)." If you're marrying a Jew, the odds are still great that you're marrying a Reform Jew. They're modern. There are over 2 million Reform Jews in the U.S. in about 850 congregations or, again according to Pew, about 35% of all Jews, making it far and away the largest Jewish denomination.

Reconstructionism is an outgrowth of the Conservative movement, founded by rabbi Mordecai Kaplan, as an effort to regenerate and revitalize Judaism by taking a middle road between Conservative and Reform. The emphasis is not so much on God as it is on being Jewish. The mission statement says that Judaism is the evolving civilization of the Jewish people. The key word is evolving which means that change is good. The problem, however, is in getting the congregation to agree on which changes. In a Reconstructing Judaism temple, democracy is the key word. Many share power and the congregation takes responsibility for all important decisions. The rabbi is a teacher, not a demagogue. I know of one Reconstructionist temple that broke apart over the question of recognizing the rights of the Palestinians. Detractors say that Reconstructing Judaism threatens Jewish identify by their acceptance of other traditions. There are only about 60,000 Reconstructionists, but the movement is growing.

CHAPTER 4

HOW TO BEHAVE
ON JEWISH HOLIDAYS

IN MY CHRISTIAN upbringing, there was Christmas, Easter and that was about it for holidays with a religious flavor. Eating, of course, is the central activity of most holidays. The rituals associated with eating during those two big celebrations were pretty minimal for us Christians. For Italians, a calzone at Easter is obligatory. At Christmas, the menu was impressive but never uniform. On non-religious holidays, however, most Americans have become accustomed to a variety of special treats: turkey at Thanksgiving, pumpkin pie on Halloween, the Fourth of July bar-b-q and beer on St. Patrick's day (which I have always thought of as an Irish, not a religious holiday). Nor was I raised with any particular ceremony to go with the holiday, other than a brief prayer of thanksgiving that we called "saying grace," but you were supposed to do that at every meal.

Jewish holiday celebrations are very different. Food, as usual, is at the heart of the event. Some of the food is special for the particular holiday (more on that later). What's really different, though, is the accompanying ceremony. Jews actually read the story of Passover and talk about what they're celebrating (you've heard of the Four Questions?). At *Chanukah*, they actually light the candles as a symbol of the religious significance of the day. And they sing the songs associated with that feast, except on *Yom Kippur* which is the somber holiday, with fasting, and nobody is supposed to be upbeat about anything.

It is very common for gentiles to be invited to a Jewish household to join in the celebration. In our house, we always make sure that, if there are parts to be read, everybody has a part. If there are gifts to give, everybody gets one. If there are songs to sing, we make copies for everybody.

What do you take as a gift? Your Jewish partner or friend may wish to take something Jewish (like *challah* or wine or Jewish cookies) but, speaking as a fellow non-member of the tribe, I wouldn't tempt the fates by taking something that you think will please because it *is* Jewish. A gentile friend once bought an expensive *mezuzah* (see the dictionary for details but it's basically a small prayer object you nail to the front door to show that you're Jewish) to his future in-laws and it was a big mistake. He was only trying to show that he knew what the thing was and that he thought it was cool but it was way too personal and completely inappropriate for a gentile.

If you're invited to a Jewish home for dinner, take what you would ordinarily take. If you're invited for a major holiday, ask your host/hostess what to bring. Sometimes, it's nice to take something from your own culture if it fits the occasion. A plate, a glass, a cup, a bread-basket, something of fabric or candlesticks that say something about you. Don't go overboard with this and don't take an Easter egg, corn muffins, or regular bread to Passover or Santa Claus to Chanukah. If you can't think of anything, a bottle of wine is fine but nobody drinks that god-awful Manishewitz Jewish wine anymore.

Rosh Hashanah

This is Jewish New Year. You've got your Gregorian Year, your fiscal year, your academic year, and the Jewish year. Judaism operates on a whole different calendar, dating, supposedly, from the time of creation. The year is based on the moon, not the sun. Jews seem to know that but very few can tell you what year it is. The year 2021 is

5781. Though it's New Year, it's not a time for champagne and noise-makers but rather for reflection on the year past.

Rosh Hashanah and *Yom Kippur*, together are called the High Holy Days, sometimes called High Holidays and none of it has anything to do with marijuana. The ten days between *Rosh Hashanah* and *Yom Kippur* are called the Days of Awe. Like New Years Day, no particular event occurred on *Rosh Hashanah*. Symbolically, it represents the day of the creation of the world. It's a time to think of what you have done this past year, to apologize where appropriate, and to make resolutions for the new year. In Jewish neighborhoods, you can see groups of the observant walking on bridges over water. There, they empty their pockets, symbolically casting off their sins.

Rosh Hashanah is a two-day celebration. It starts in mid to late September – changes every year. Like all Jewish holidays, it starts at sundown the day before because of a teaching in Genesis. The New Year service usually gets the biggest attendance at temple. *Yom Kippur* is a close second.

For gentiles new to the service, it's a lot like a regular *shabbes* service. The *shofar*, or ram's horn, is sounded several times to open and close the High Holidays, or "Days of Awe." Isaac, the son of Abraham, was spared from sacrifice when God ordered Abraham to kill this ram that was stuck in a thicket near the spot of the sacrifice. The ram (and its horn), the teaching goes, thus speak directly to God. In today's *Rosh Hashanah* services, it is an honor to be called to blow the shofar in the name of the fight against evil and injustice.

Before services, greet everyone with *gut yontif* which means something like "good day" or "have a good holy day." After services, you can just say happy new year or, more commonly, *l'shana tova,* which means "have a good and sweet new year."

If you are then retiring to the *Rosh Hashanah* dinner, you will eat apples dipped in honey to symbolically express the hope that there will be many sweet times in the coming year (more on that later).

The Shofar

Yom Kippur

Yom Kippur is the climax to the High Holy Days. It is a day of atonement. Jews do not go to work or school. It's a day of complete rest. Many will fast. And don't say *good shabbes*. During the ten days between the two holidays, Jews are supposed to repent, pray and do acts of charity so as to tilt the scales of their lives toward the good for the coming year. *Yom Kippur* is as close as Jews get to the Christian idea of the confession of sins. The most obvious difference is that, in Jewish, you don't confess to anyone in particular, much less in a private audience with a hidden priest or minister. The other big difference is that, in Jewish, God doesn't forgive for merely confessing the sin and saying prayers as "penance." The Jewish sinner must also atone for the sins and commit to change and leading a better life.

Kol Nidre is the prayer service that starts *Yom Kippur*. It's Hebrew for "all vows." It is held just before sunset on *Yom Kippur* which, with *Rosh Hashanah,* is the most crowded service of the year in synagogue. I learned the hard way that men will wear jackets and ties to *Kol Nidre* and women will dress up – conservatively. The color is white (definitely optional) to symbolize the freshness and simplicity of the service and the new year. The prayers themselves are chanted three times to clear the slate between you and God. Figuring prominently are the *Yizkor*, a memorial prayer, and the *Avodah*, a prayer remembering the sacrifices since the destruction of the Temple. The most solemn, sometimes haunting, of all Jewish prayers are usually sung by the Cantor. The service evokes the ageless oppression of the Jews and symbolically begins the dialogue with God for the coming year. Whether you understand the service or not, I think you will find it very touching.

Fasting on *Yom Kippur* is important to very many Jews. The last meal should be in the late afternoon, just before the evening of *Yom Kippur* service. No food should be taken until sunset the following day. Many people will stay in temple all day on *Yom Kippur* and break the fast together.

Passover

This, the oldest Jewish holiday, is called *pesach* and the ceremony is called a *seder*. Passover dates from the escape of the children of Israel from Egypt about 3000 years ago (see the Jewish history chapter). In a sense, Passover represents salvation to the Jews in the same way that the Resurrection represents salvation to the Christian. Remember, the Last Supper of Christ was really a Passover dinner.

The Passover *seder* occurs in the home (the largest Jewish in-home celebration) and is the one where a gentile is most likely to be invited. Passover 2020, of course, was affected by the coronavirus and most Jews did "zoom *seders*" with people tuning in remotely to read the prayers and eat "together." There were a couple of positives to that experience: you could invite anyone you wanted from around the world. It was great to see people you wouldn't ordinarily see. Also, the zoom *seders* were much more open to discussion since the meal itself couldn't really be "shared." When you got to the part where people would start running around serving the various courses, the remote *seders* I experienced (and there were three) just turned into discussion groups fueled by cups of wine.

Passover lasts eight days, although most Jews only celebrate the first two nights. It occurs anytime from late March until mid-April, often coming right near Easter. In my house, we have lots of different celebrations.

There is required reading for the Passover *Seder*, but you don't have to read it in advance. The text that is read at the *seder* dinner is called the *Haggadah*. It's the narrative of Israel's bondage and flight from Egypt over 3000 years ago, as recounted in Exodus. The *Haggadah* contains all the prayers, hymns and songs for Passover. Some Jews assemble their own *Haggadahs* from various sources to reflect the theme they want to emphasize or to include particular songs and prayers. For many years, we have held what we somewhat pretentiously call a "freedom *seder*," tying the Jews flight from Egypt to contemporary battles for freedom. Our *Haggadah* is a patchwork document, constantly changing, yet preserving the essentials of the service. For example, Susan wrote a passage about her Jewish up-bringing that she reads every year. It's a creative exercise in which, in a sense, you construct your own theology. At any *seder*, however, the key moment is always when you get to the Four Questions and the youngest at the table asks why this night is different from every other night. Otherwise, we change the songs, we encourage people to tell their own stories and we laugh.

Another important *seder* event is when a piece of *matzoh* called the *afikomen* is hidden. Later in the meal, the kids will all go run and look for it. A prize, usually money, is given to the finder. From what I can tell, this is done to keep the kids awake with anticipation. At another point, early, the door is opened so that Elijah, the prophet, can enter, announce the coming of the Messiah, and drink the cup of wine that is reserved for him. As my younger son once asked: "Are we letting that ghost in again this year?" Check the cup of wine periodically to see if Elijah drank any. Some progressive Jews, in the interest of inclusion, will leave a glass of water for Miriam, the sister of Moses. It is said that Miriam's Well was the source of water for the Israelites in the desert.

Pulling together the *seder* meal is a substantial undertaking. First there are all the symbolic foods, with a sample of each put into a special, usually ornate *seder* plate. *Matzah* (which you know is flat and cracker-like with no yeast commemorating the Exodus from Egypt when there was no time to let the bread rise), *charoset* (a really tasty mixture of nuts, apples, cinnamon and other stuff), *maror* (bitter herbs to remind of the bondage in Egypt; don't eat them), *karpas* (a sprig of parsley symbolizing the life in nature), a cooked egg (*beitzah*- a symbol of mourning over the destruction of the temple), and a shank bone of roast lamb (the *zeroalt*, symbolizing the hasty eating of lamb before the Exodus). Many modern Jews will add the orange as a gesture of solidarity with Jewish women, gays, lesbians, and marginalized peoples. It supposedly came from a rabbi's comment once that "women belong on the *bima* like an orange belongs on the *seder* plate." That explanation has been denied on all sides. Regardless, the symbol remains in many Jewish homes. The *seder* plate is passed around the table and everybody takes a little of everything. To this point, you will be very unimpressed with the food.

The Seder Plate

Then, the wine. You need a lot because there are four points in the *Haggadah* that call for the drinking of a cup. Most Jews have stopped using that wretched sweet wine and have switched to the New York Times recommended list. Then, there's the meal: *matzah* ball soup, *gefilte* fish (this is ground, deboned whitefish served in a lump with horseradish; it's an acquired taste), the brisket (an essential for Jewish meat eaters; usually slow cooked to tenderness, *au jus*, and with vegetables), the *kugel* (a sweet egg noodle casserole), the whole works. You will be feeling much better by now. For dessert, let your imagination run wild: macaroons are traditional as are flourless cakes of all kinds. But I looked up some dessert recipes and there really are an infinite number of Passover desserts (see the food section).

The whole spirit of *pesach* is to invite a bunch of people, especially ones who have no place to go on *pesach*, and to celebrate the revolt against tyranny and the liberation of the oppressed, no matter what nationality or religion. In our house, we have invited a mixed bag of people including a Catholic priest, a Palestinian, a healthy number of atheists and a lot of friends in mixed marriages. We always have a majority or near-majority of gentiles at the table. We encourage everyone to bring their traditions with them to share, whether it be a story, a prayer, or a song. There is a leader who calls on everybody else to read a portion of the *Haggadah*. At the appropriate points, everybody stops and eats from the *seder* plate or drinks wine or sings a song and then back to the *Haggadah*. "*Dayeinu*" and "*Zum Galli Galli*" are always on the set list. It's a loud and festive occasion. Toward the end of the feast, everybody says "Next year in Jerusalem." In my house, we say "Next year in Jerusalem and then maybe we'll take a nice cruise."

Chanukah (or Hannukah)

The events memorialized by *Chanukah* are really not that important in Jewish history. Many think that *Chanukah* has been made a bigger deal than it is as an antidote to Christmas. *Chanukah* usually precedes Christmas by a week or two. It's another celebration of the struggle against oppression that has marked all of Jewish history. The abbreviated story is as follows: In 175 B.C., the conquering Syrians ordered the Jewish Maccabees to convert to Greek polytheism. Antiochus IV, King of the Syrians, ordered the Jews to build altars and shrines for idols, to stop circumcising male babies, and to stop celebrating Jewish holidays. He also burned the books of the Jews and killed anyone (women and children included) who would not bow to Zeus in the Great Temple (reportedly a beautiful building of cedar and polished granite).

Many Jews fled to live in caves. In 167 B.C., the Syrians met with Mattathias, a respected Jewish holy man, to get him to eat pork and visit the altar to Zeus. He refused. He even killed a Hebrew traitor who had been enticed by the promise of riches. Mattathias then tore down the altar and headed to the hills. He and his son, Judah the Maccabee, led an uprising of Jews against the Syrians, fighting and eventually winning a three-year guerilla war, against all odds. When the Jews returned to Jerusalem in triumph in 165 B.C., they began the process of restoring the Temple, which had been sacked. One *menorah* that had not been destroyed was found to have one drop of oil in it. The drop made a candle burn for eight days. This miracle inspired the Jews who then restored the temple and celebrated its rededication with a weeklong festival of lights.

The *menorah* has become the symbol of *Chanukah*. For eight days in December, Jews will light one more candle on the menorah every night. There are nine candles on the menorah (some have seven but I have no idea why that is), one for each night of *Chanukah* and the one in middle called the *shammash*, which is used to light the others, one for the passing of each day of Chanukah. Take the *shammash* and start by putting a candle in the rightmost position. The next night, use the *shammash* to light the first candle again and to light a new candle to the left of the one lit the nights before and continue that way until, on the final night, all the candles are lit. It's an honor to be asked to light a candle. Children are customarily given small presents on each night of *Chanukah*. It's fine for non-Jewish guests to give these small presents (a book, a game, a small toy). It's nothing like the one-day Christmas orgy, but it's fun nonetheless. The children are also given *Chanukah gelt*, which can be cash but is usually those wrapped chocolate coins. There is a prayer that is said at the lighting of the candles and a Chanukah song or two that can be sung. Smaller children also play a game with a spinning top called Dreydls.

Dreydls

Then you eat. A traditional Chanukah meals includes *latkes*, which are small fried potato pancakes which you eat by the dozen, sometimes with applesauce.

All gentiles should remember that most Jews, practicing or not, feel a little like strangers in a strange land around Christmas. Jewish children must have a very hard time dealing with all the Santa Claus hype. No Christmas tree, no reindeer, etc. On Christmas day, Jews go to the movies. If Jewish families celebrate Christmas at all, it's not from infidelity to their faith but rather because of that great sucking sound that begins sometime even before Halloween known as the market force of Christmas.

Purim

Purim is the party holiday. Very relaxed, not a lot of rules, and very much oriented toward the kids. It happens in the early spring (March-April) and lasts for one day. It celebrates a victory by the Persian Jews over yet another king who wanted to kill them. Here's the whole *megillah,* as described in one of the books of Esther which is read at Pruim, but in short form.

King Ahashverosh of Persia had an advisor named Haman. The King fell in love with and married a nice Jewish girl named Esther. Esther's uncle (some say cousin) Mordechai refused to bow before Haman because Jews bow only to God, not to people. Haman was furious and told the King to have all the Jews killed. The day of death was to be determined by drawing lots: *purim* in Persian. The King agreed, not knowing or having forgotten that his wife was Jewish. Esther came out, refreshed his recollection and convinced the King to spare the Jews and hang Haman.

So, Purim celebrates the courage of Esther and the evil of Haman. The synagogue service is filled with kids who are allowed to scream as loudly as they want, stomp their feet and shake noisemakers every time Haman's name is mentioned and the story of Esther is read. The kids (and usually their parents) dress in costumes and put on plays and tell stories, all of which are supposed to be at least vaguely related to Esther. On this feast, you heat *hammentashen,* which are triangle-shaped cookies filled with poppy seeds or fruit, symbolizing the shape of Haman's ears.

CHAPTER 5

HOW TO BEHAVE AT OTHER IMPORTANT JEWISH CEREMONIES

IN THE LAST chapter, we discussed the most important Jewish holidays. In this chapter, we take a look at the ceremonies accompanying life events that are personal but common to all families: birth, wedding, death. If Jewish, add the ceremony that marks the passage into adulthood: the *bar* or *bat mitzvah*. It's probably the most distinctive of all Jewish family ceremonies, kind of like the *quince anos* fiesta for Latin girls passing into womanhood, or the piercing of young Native American men with eagle claws to mark the passage into manhood. For Catholics, there's Confirmation when the child is about 12 years old but it doesn't have the same *cachet* as the others.

There are several "womb to tomb" ceremonies you should understand in case you're invited to participate:

The Bris

The rite of initiation into the human race for the Christian child is the Baptism. You buy the baby a white gown, pick the godparents, invite all the relatives, go to the church, pour water on the baby's head while saying the prayers, and call it a day. The *bris* should only be so easy. If you have the misfortune of being born a male Jewish child, you will, practically by the end of your first week, have been subject to a controlled mutilation of your sexual organ and, not to be forgotten, you'll be forced to consume alcohol. That's a little overstated but let's just says it's a good thing they don't give the babies a choice of religion.

The ceremony of the *bris* is held on the eighth day after the birth of a male child, even if that day falls on *shabbes*. The purpose is to celebrate the arrival of a male and the covenanting of that child with the Jewish community. As with all traditionally patriarchal societies, the arrival of a son is a greater blessing than the arrival of a daughter. The fact that the *bris* is for boys only is a vestige of that tradition.

The Jewishness of the *bris* is central to the integrity of the ceremony. A mixed couple would not have a *bris* one day and a baptism the next, regardless of how much they intend to expose the child to both traditions. One excludes the other. You cannot have a real *bris* without declaring the child to be a child of Abraham. By the same token, I don't imagine a priest or minister would conduct a baptism without acceptance of Jesus Christ. In our family, we tried to have a "non-religious" *bris* for each of our boys but we realized that, without the prayers of the *mohel* (pronounced MOY-el) who leads the ceremony, the *bris* loses all its character. Character, shmaracter, why do I have to see it?

The ritual dates back to Genesis. It is the oldest rite in the Jewish religion. The first patriarch, Abraham, was commanded to do the nasty on himself when he was ninety-nine years old. Then he was told to do it to his son Isaac who was already 13 years old and probably had no idea what was up as his father approached him with a sharp stone.

When the child is a girl, many Jews (not the Orthodox) will have naming ceremonies called the *brit* (or *b'rit*). Recently, new ceremonies have been drawn up to welcome the female child. I haven't been to any yet but it appears that the parents are encouraged to make a statement at the ceremony as to why the particular name was chosen, in addition to the usual prayers. The child ordinarily will have a Hebrew name as well as a given name that she will carry through life. The ceremony is held anytime in the first month of life. At either ceremony, the family and friends are invited but, as celebrations go, it's pretty free form – as long as there is food.

Why am I avoiding what actually happens at a *bris*? It's a circumcision. Most non-Jewish newborn males were circumcised as a health precaution but under more antiseptic conditions and not right in front of me. In Genesis 17:11, however, it is mandated that all Jewish males be circumcised on the eighth day to serve as a perpetual reminder of the covenant between Abraham and God. There must be a better way to memorialize the deal. On the positive side, the ceremony itself is mercifully short and painful (for the parents, that is a certainty; one can only speculate at the degree of "discomfort" experienced by the baby).

Only sadists should take a front row seat. Two candles are lit in the *bris* room. A chair is set up for Elijah the prophet who will protect the infant from danger. Though godmothers and godfathers are no longer common at the bris, if the ceremony is being done by the books, the mother and baby will be in another room with the godmother. The father designates a man to go get them. That man is usually the godfather. He takes the baby from the mother and gives it to the godmother who brings the baby into the *bris* room and everybody stands and says "Blessed be he who cometh." The *mohel* (a practicing Jew with special training in surgical skills) takes the baby, says a prayer, hands the baby to the father who hands it to another person called a *sandek* who will actually hold the baby in his or her lap to keep the baby still on the table during the circumcision. The father says a prayer and the *mohel* does the dirty deed. Not only did I not say a prayer at either of my boys' *bris*, I don't think I even opened by eyes. My wife says that, for the second one, I left the room. The *mohel* puts a drop of wine on a piece of gauze and puts it in the baby's mouth as anesthetic. The thing is done with a scalpel. A scalpel. Then, the *mohel* does some blessings, pronounces the baby's Hebrew name and everybody eats, including the baby who is on the mother's breast.

Speaking of names, most Jews are given a Hebrew name. The *Ashkenazim* sect usually follows the rule that you do not name a child after a living relative. The child of *Ashkenazic* Jews usually receives two names: a Hebrew name after a dead relative and a name common to English and the United States. The *Sephardim*, another Jewish grouping, usually follow a different rule that is more like the Italian Catholic tradition I experienced. The first male is named after the paternal grandfather, the second male after the maternal grandfathers, the first female after the paternal grandmother, the second female after the maternal grandmother.

Under Jewish law, any child born of a Jewish mother is Jewish. If the mother is gentile, she needs to convert if the child is to be Jewish under Jewish law. The orthodox don't recognize converts.

By the way, the *mohel* will cost some money. My boys were only five years apart but the fees went up 100%.

Bar/Bat Mitzvahs

So, you've been to baptisms. If you're Catholic, maybe you got your First Communion. Maybe you were "confirmed" when you were 12. But, trust me, you've never seen anything like the *Bar or Bat Mitzvah*. In fact, even most weddings cannot compare to the work, the meticulous planning, the show, and the overall psychological trauma on the entire family of the *Bar or Bat Mitzvah*.

The *Bar Mitzvah* ceremony will take place at a regular synagogue service on shabbes and as close to the *Bar Mitzvah* boy's 13th birthday as can be arranged. The *Bat Mitzvah*, for girls, can occur when the girl is 12 because girls reach maturity faster than boys. Actually, the *Bat Mitzvah* is a 20th Century invention, the first one having been held in New York City in 1922. The Commentaries in the *Talmud*, it is said, were never intended to be applied to women.

The *Bar/Bat Mitzvah* is planned several years in advance. The details are spelled out later in this chapter. At this point, suffice it to say that we reserved our date at the synagogue when our child was nine years old.

The purpose of the *Bar/Bat Mitzvah* is to call the child to the *Torah*, to formally admit him or her to the Jewish community and to grant the privilege of reciting the prophetic portion of the *Torah* (called the *haftarah*). The parents place a *tallit* around the child's shoulders to symbolize the moment when the child assumes the duty to conduct his or her own life but to observe the laws of Judaism.

Normally, the ceremony takes place in the synagogue. Be forewarned, these services tend to go on a bit, especially if it's Orthodox. And a lot of it is in Hebrew. I don't think it's a sign of disrespect to say that, unless it's your kid, these things get pretty boring. First, the family members will all come up and say short prayers that are special for that particular day of the year, just as the Gospel at mass is also on an annual cycle. The male family members can usually do the prayer in Hebrew. The father of the barmitzvee (that's not Jewish) will recite a prayer in Hebrew giving thanks for being free from responsibility for the child's future actions (if only that were true). "Praised is the one who has freed me from the responsibility for this child's actions." Even if the *bar mitzvah* kid has been adopted or the natural father is no longer married to the natural mother, it is still the natural father who recites this prayer. A non-Jewish father is not called to the *Torah* even if he has learned the blessings in Hebrew. The gentile father will stand on the *bima* and just give a little speech.

At some point, the bar mitzvee starts the readings from the *haftarah*. Part of the readings will be sung or chanted. These readings must be long enough to show that the *bar/mitzvah* has studied the Hebrew long and well. Most kids race through it as fast as they can and, generally, without enthusiasm. The child's real prayer is that this be over as quickly as possible. After all, at that age, who wants to have the whole place looking at you and deciding what kind of job you're doing? If a kid does a dramatic reading, the parents are looking at paying for law school.

The rabbi will say lots of prayers and the cantor will sing some songs. As usual, the congregation joins in the responsive readings. Gentiles are free to join in. Think of the ceremony as a little like the Oscar award ceremony: lots of presentations, interspersed with a few songs and production numbers and everybody thanking everybody. Sometimes the temple will double-dip and do two *bar/bat mitzvahs* in the same service. So then you have two families and two kids to listen to. Near the end of the service, the rabbi or the President of the congregation will give the kid a certificate and a gift which is usually something appropriate either from Israel or to be used in Israel.

The importance of the *bar/bat mitzvah* cannot be over-estimated. This is hard for the non-Jew to understand. It's a lot different than the gentile confirmation or any graduation or any of the other familiar transition points. Read how one Jewish parent, in kind of free form, describes her son's *bar mitzvah:*

> It was outrageous! Absolutely outrageous! I mean, every piece of it. You have the kid in the middle and all the different pieces that make up a person, all the different spokes, it touches on all of them. You know how to make somebody a whole, full individual....it made me proud about my parents being Jewish, my grandparents, I mean it was a real sense

of connection with the past and with the future. I know that there were generations and generations of people and relatives that really suffered and sacrificed so that we could live so freely and openly. So I was proud of that, and proud that we could pass that on, that tradition, onto our son. And he could feel a sense of that connection and just being another link in the whole process, the whole chain of Jews.

Ten Things to Do at the Bar/Bat Mitzvah to Avoid Falling Asleep

1. Look at the Bible in front of your seat and practice reading back to front. It's good literature. You'll be a better person for it and it's probably the only time you'll look at it.

2. Check out the family (they sit mostly together in the first couple of rows). Predict which one will cry first when they do the family readings. Try to count how many times the mother will mouth the words "slow down." Evaluate how personal the testimonials to the bar mitzvee are. Guess whether 90-year-old Great Uncle Harry will make it to the podium and get through the reading without something embarrassing happening. Give an imaginary prize for the most original hair color.

3. Grade the kid and his/her performance in categories such as a) style, b) presentation, c) voice projection, d) sincerity, e) singing ability, and f) originality in the thank yous. Extra points for humor but don't tell the kid any of this.

4. Check out the friends of the *bar/bat mitzvah* kid. They invariably sit together in the back two or three rows. At 13, the girls are way more mature and much taller than the boys who still look very uncomfortalbe in their little suits.

5. Project onto the mindset of the rabbi or cantor. Surely they know that 90% of these kids will wind up coming to temple once a year.

6. Guess the professions of the assembled guests. Remember, you can never overestimate the number of lawyers. I'm just sayin…. At the party, have a close family member give you the answers.

7. You can go to the bathroom, but only once.

8. Predict what will be on the dessert table at the party. It will be more than you can imagine.

9. Guess what the table decorations at the party will be.

10. Practice saying *"Mazel tov."*

Services are usually followed by a luncheon that is a sharing of wine and bread and a prayer that may or may not be followed by a lavish celebration either later in the afternoon or that evening. A state-of-the-art *bar/bat mitzvah* is like a wedding in its scope and design. A beautiful hall has been rented, the food catered, and the tables decorated. If you're really doing it up, each table will have a center-piece. A Jewish theme would be pictures of the Old City of Jerusalem. Boring. At my nephew's *bar mitzvah*, every table had an athletic shoe filled with baseball cards as a souvenir centerpiece to symbolize his great love of sports. We took two and saved some money. Others will choose bouquets of flowers or balloons with pictures of the family. At one recent celebration I attended, the kids' table was literally cov-ered with a bottomless pit of all kinds of candy. They wouldn't let me sit there. Most *bar/bat mitzvahs* and weddings include the distinctly Jewish custom of the sweet table. No such thing as a simple dessert, like a *Torah* cake. It's a whole new spread of cakes, cookies, pies, fruit, ice cream, lots of chocolate – maybe fountains of chocolate. If you're invited to one of these, your diet goes on a holiday.

There will also be a *bar/bat mitzvah* band (or a DJ) and all of the kid's friends dancing and doing the limbo and all that. The *Bar Mitzvah* boy or the *Bat Mitzvah* girl is expected to work the tables, greeting all the friends of their parents and every great aunt or third cousin they didn't know they had. Some they will dance with. It's a lot of pressure for a kid barely a teenager.

All the guests give The Star an envelope, which is the *gelt*, and it is absolutely *de rigueur* to tell the kid, preferably in the presence of the parents, what a wonderful reading that was of the *haftarah*. The parents may hope that the kid makes as much money in gifts as they spent for the temple and the personalized T-shirts they handed out at the celebration. In a sense, it's a ritualized transfer of wealth.

At some point in the celebration, there will be a lighting of seven candles by close relatives who will be called to the table by the barvitzee who will precede their arrival with a little speech about how much it means to have everyone there for the celebration. The parents will also get a few words in. The hired videographer duly records all of this. Dancing, eating and leaning on the open bar are, however, the principal activities of the celebration. A good time can truly be had by all.

Before describing *Bar Mitzvah* planning in detail, I want to mention a growing phenomenon in Reform Judaism: the confirmation as a substitute for the *Bar or Bat Mitzvah*. These services are usually held during the child's fifteenth or sixteenth year, on the holiday of *Shavuot* which commemorates the giving of the *Torah*. I haven't seen any stats on how widespread the confirmation practice has become but a number of commentaries conclude that it is growing or even "revolutionizing" Reform Judaism. As true as that may be, many Reform Jews still do the *Bar or Bat Mitzvah*. In fact, a Jewish guy I met one night on the subway jokingly told me the three ways to distinguish a Reform *Bar/Bat Mitzvah* from any other:

1) the *haftarah* readings are in English;
2) the blessing at the luncheon is "They tried to conquer us, they couldn't, let's eat!
3) the main course at the luncheon is crab claws.

Notice how Reform Jews get no respect.

You Think It's Hard Planning a Wedding? Try Making a *Bar/Bat Mitzvah*

There are many, many different ways to make a *Bar/Bat Mitzvah*. None of them are cheap. Double the price if you're from New York. The larger and fancier they get, the more *tsouris* there is for the planners. If you think I'm being over-the-top in my description, be sure to see the movie "Keeping Up with the Steins (2006)." Let's get started. The following timeline is typical for the mid to upper range event.

TWO YEARS IN ADVANCE

1. go to the temple and check out possible dates for the *Bar/ Bat Mitzvah*. Some congregations will have a meeting of all

the fifth grade parents to give them a jump-start on an event that will occur usually at the end of the seventh grade year. Pick a date but it's not going to be the kid's 13th birthday or even the Saturday closest to the birthday. That date is taken. You may even be asked to share a date. That means your kid and somebody else's kid will do a double service, which, of course, means that not all the light shines on your child, and your guests get to sit through an extended service.

2. Conceptualize. Will it be a service followed by a full lunch, a service followed by a light sharing of bread (*kiddush*) and a party that night, a lunch and a party, a lunch for the grown-ups and party for the kids? You need a model. The kid will be most concerned about the friends part. Will there be a band, a DJ, other forms of entertainment (I remember the bat mitzvah with the full band, an emcee, and a dance team to make noise and put on a show)? Will the invitees include everybody you ever met or just a circle of your 100-200 closest friends and relatives? In other words, whose party is this anyway? Start checking out places for the reception, the luncheon and or the party on that Saturday night. Do you have family far away? Start thinking about hotel and reception in the same place.

This conceptualizing process goes on throughout the year. Usually, it's a collective process, involving the children, family, the in-laws, friends and neighbors. It can easily become yet another source of family conflict. How to make the *bar/bat mitzvah* ranks right up there in the life cycle with what college should I go to, the wedding, and whether we move to the suburbs. I definitely recommend lining up a therapist.

ONE YEAR IN ADVANCE

By now, it's time to start:
1. Making room reservations; that includes the reception hall at

the synagogue, the restaurant or hotel for the party, the block of rooms at the hotel for out-of-towners, etc. Does the hall provide all the tables and linens? Add rental agencies to the list. And don't forget the buses to get the hotel people to the event. And the welcome-baskets for every hotel room.

2. Doing drafts of the guest list; which cousin will be offended if not invited? Which cousin will be offended if his kids are not invited?

3. Choosing a caterer(s) and the kind of food and drink you want. There are the main courses (remember, kids menu is different than the adults), the various types of drink, and then there's the dessert table – each of which is a separate pain in the neck. Dear friends of ours once invited us to their home on two Sunday nights to sample a variety of white and red wines to help decide which they should order for the Saturday night party (I voted for the alcoholic ones). If the party is at the hotel, they will only allow certain outside caterers (if any) and don't even think about open bar for the whole night unless you've hit the lottery.

4. The party: This is not easy. Some people hire a party planner, just like for weddings. If you do that, you don't have to worry about a lot of things, like choosing a band or DJ. The leader of the band or the DJ usually acts as the emcee of the evening, doing all the introductions, choosing the appropriate time for the music, the moment to join the kids with the old people, when to do the candles, the conga line, when to dance the *hora* – just to name a few (make sure to give the DJ your own play list too). If you have a coordinator or planner, he/she will give the music leader an actual script, sometimes called an "itinerary," that times out every party event. Some DJ's or bands bring a whole dance team with them. Those folks are usually friends from the athletic club moonlighting on weekends. Do you want this party to be ear-splitting loud and totally active with everybody *shvitz-*

ing through their clothes or do you want people to be able to have conversations? Or do you want the music and the tables in separate rooms? Do you want something Jewish, like a *klezmer* band or was there enough of that stuff at the service? Hell, you can hire the Cirque du Soleil if you want to. The possibilities are endless. I have only touched the tip of the music/noise iceberg.

5. Some of the other things you or your coordinator may have to deal with: balloon towers at the entrance to the party room, goodie bags for the kids when they leave, dance prizes, dealing with the kitchen (vegetarians, low-salt, gluten-free, etc. etc.), the roving photographers, collecting the envelopes, making sure the music keeps the kids busy during adult cocktails and then again during the salad course, and listening to Cousin Ruth who has to eat early to relieve the babysitter who's not getting along with her little Jeffrey. It's hard to imagine the parents having a good time.

SIX TO EIGHT MONTHS IN ADVANCE

1) The invitations. A *Bar/Bat Mitzvah* invitation is not to be trifled with. It's not something that comes off the computer graphics pages. First, you look at the invitation books. You make at least basic decisions: the look, the general text, the budget. Then you call the "invitations lady" recommended by your synagogue or party planner. She will help you work on the text of the invitation but she wants basic information herself: how many? Do you want a separate card for the reception or just include it with the service (meaning: are you inviting different people?) Are you going to include a preprinted stamped return envelope (for the RSVPs) or will you do it by Evite? What color ink? Lined envelopes? Multiple layers? Remember, words in Hebrew are extra as is text in the lower right and left corner of the invitation. How about folding? Do you want self-mailing envelopes that play "My *Yiddishe* Mama" when opened (I don't make this stuff up)? When they come back, are you going to have the mailing addresses printed

or hire a calligrapher? The invitation lady will identify resources for everything you've chosen and put the order in.

2) The envelopes all have to be stuffed and sent out a respectable 6-8 weeks in advance. This means you have to decide whom to invite at least several months in advance. The potential for family conflict is mindboggling. You can cave in and invite every second cousin you've never seen and their dates and then take out another mortgage on the house. Or, you can invite just the parents, or the parents and older kids only, or just the families of first cousins, or only fiancés that you know or whatever line you choose to draw in the sand. And how do you tell your ex-spouse that some part of his/her family is not invited? For those on the bubble, be prepared to call them to tactfully explain your position and then be prepared for them to never speak to you again.

You can avoid a lot of this by setting up a *bar/bat mitzvah* website with all the essential information and you can use one of the on-line services like E-event to deal with invitations and RSVPs. But some people consider that tacky.

3) The service booklet. This is the hand-out to all the synagogue guests that describes the service and talks about the kid and who the various relatives are who ascend the *bima*. This can be a lovely statement about your family, your values, your child's development and your joy at having everyone join in the celebration. It can also be a horrible experience, leading to the rending of garments and loss of hair. The kid will treat this as homework, especially at a point when the event doesn't even seem real. The booklet, of course, has to be printed. See above about the invitations.

4) Did I neglect to mention that the kid is now studying with the rabbi, the cantor and maybe a tutor, learning the chosen portion of the *haftorah* in Hebrew and the singing of the prayers? The child also has to write a short statement of what this event means to him/her and thanking all the appropriate parties. In addition, the child is supposed to do what is known as a *tzedakah* or service project. At a recent *bar mitzvah*, the child had devised a new recycling system for the

synagogue. Other children will work with seniors, the homeless, or some other deserving group. The child is encouraged to be creative.

WITHIN SIX MONTHS OF THE EVENT

1) The theme. That's right. The theme. One of the many issues you don't face when planning a wedding. Many families offer the child the opportunity to express a unifying theme to the *bar/bat mitzvah* party. It could be baseball, "we are the world," Southeast Asian cultures – almost anything. There's no requirement of a theme and, certainly, some families think it makes the event more of a spectacle. If there is a theme, however, it has consequences: the centerpieces. Usually tied to the theme and, of course, to the colors in the room. Each party table will have a display that reflects either the theme or something equally appropriate, like the child's service project or maybe just the child doing charming things.

2) Clothing. Enough said.

3) Photographer, videographer, or both. This requires more than six months if you plan to present, as a "featurette," a short, well-edited video with good production values about the child's incredibly successful life so far. Videos with music, snapshots, old home videos, Instagram posts, short speeches – all the stuff that a suffering parent has spent countless hours collecting and marking to give to the professionals. These videos are for the high-end party. Almost everybody has a video guy, equipped to catch not only the kid dancing with her grandfather but also ready to go table to table, asking people to offer their personal congratulations.

4) Floral arrangements. You know what I mean.

5) The seating chart. Don't get me started. When you arrive, you find your name on a little card that tells you where to sit. If there is a head table or an "immediate family," everybody will judge how they rate by their distance from that table. We have friends who had guests that objected so strongly to where they were seated that the child's father had to throw them out of the party. When devising the chart be sure to remember who is not speaking to whom, what the

pecking order of the family is (higher rank to the front), which in-laws don't get along, who hates sitting next to the air conditioners, and who can't climb stairs. You also want the candle-lighters to be near the front to save time. With non-family members, the objective is to seat people with somebody they know. So, maybe the neighborhood sits together, maybe the business contacts, maybe the old people. There's always an "oddball" table – the kid's teacher, classmates of the parents, long-lost friends, etc. Ask the hotel for a seating plan of the room. I'm not kidding.

6) The lighting of the candles. In an ideal world, the child decides who should light the thirteen candles, in what order, and what should be said in connection with each. But how would that look – the Little League coach, the gym teacher, the coolest mom of all the friends, and then the friends. You the parents have to cover all the bases, first and foremost, in the family. This was such a source of conflict and *hocking* in one family we know that they were fighting between the service and the party about the candles.

6) The extra Friday night dinner or Sunday brunch, probably at your house, for the out-of-town guests, on the theory that you'll have the energy and desire to hang out with them.

7) Did I mention the actual service? Somebody should take a few minutes with the rabbi and cantor to discuss details. Whatever.

I don't even want to talk about what you should be prepared to do the actual day of the ceremony/party. Nor will I discuss some of the things that can go wrong at the ceremony/party. Already I've probably overdone it. Overall, *Bar/Bat Mitzvahs* are wonderful events and I don't want to further de-incentivize anyone to have one.

WEDDINGS

The Council of Jewish Federations shocked the Jewish world in 1990 with their study showing that 52% of Jews who married between 1985 and 1990 married non-Jews, up from a paltry 9% in 1965. In 2013, the Pew Research Center issued a report concluding that 58% of all Jews married non-Jews and it was a whopping 71%

among the non-Orthodox. So, Jews are marrying non-Jews more than they are marrying within the tribe. So, you are going to one and probably more than one Jewish wedding, even if it's a mixed wedding. These statistics feed the argument, of course, that Judaism is being destroyed from within. I think the fear is exaggerated. Like many other ethnics who emigrated to the U.S. near the turn of the century, most Jewish adults today were raised by American-born parents in an English-speaking home, mixing with non-Jews all the time. This does not mean, however, that intermarriage means an abandonment of Judaism. Most mixed couples will agree, in advance, on key religious issues that will respect both heritages, including how to conduct the wedding service. There is still hope for Judaism as long as every Jewish mother makes it perfectly clear that she is unhappy with every non-Jewish partner, even potential ones. Like the old joke goes:

A telephone rings and the mother answers. It's her daughter.

"Mama," she says. "I'm engaged!"

"Mazeltov!" says the mother excitedly.

"You have to know something, though, Mama. He isn't Jewish."

The mother is quiet.

"We don't have any money, but he's looking for work."

"That's no problem," the mother says. "You'll come live here with Papa and me. We'll give you our bedroom."

"But where will you stay?"

"Papa will sleep on the couch in the living room."

"And what about you, Mama?"

"About me, you don't have to worry, because as soon as I get off the phone, I'm jumping out the window."

In our own case, it only took my in-laws four years to get used to the idea of having me in the family. When it finally became clear to them that I wasn't going away and, worse, that we were going to get married, there was some negotiating necessary to get their blessing.

We decided to have a mostly non-denominational wedding. No rabbi, no priest. The Judge who presided over Susan's first jury trial as a lawyer married us. A very nice man, for a judge, who, though Jewish, was not allowed to make any references to explicitly religious themes. We wrote our own vows. We got married in a hotel, which is very common. I wore a black velvet jacket (very hip in those days) and Susan wore off-white. We didn't have a big deal wedding march but most Jewish marriages do. We were married under the *huppa* (see discussion later) and I broke the glass at the end of the ceremony. Certain concessions were gladly made to Susan's parents because, after all, it was their nickel. At the reception we did both the *hora* and the *tarantella*. I had a great time. Susan doesn't remember it at all. After all, it was open bar. Those Diet Cokes, straight and on the rocks, will do it every time.

Here are the rules: first of all, no weddings on the Sabbath, i.e. Friday sundown to Saturday sundown, or on major holidays. So that means it'll probably be Saturday night or Sunday. Orthodox and Conservative also prohibit weddings before or during certain other holidays or days of particular religious significance. The wedding can be held in a synagogue, a club, a restaurant, a hotel or somebody's home. A Jewish couple can be married by a justice of the peace and it'll be official. A civil marriage between a Jew and a gentile, alone, is not recognized. Orthodox and some Conservative rabbis will not officiate at mixed marriages. Reform and Reconstructionist Rabbis are much more flexible but it's always an individual decision. During the week before the marriage, Orthodox and some Conservative brides will visit a *mikva,* which is a ritual cleansing bath. Under traditional law so old that no one observes it anymore, a woman is supposed to take a mikva during every menstrual period until menopause.

The Jewish wedding ceremony occurs under a *huppa* (sometimes written *chuppah*), a canopy that is used to help celebrate "the king and queen of the day." The *huppa* symbolizes the bride's leaving her father's house for the domain of the groom. It's usually made with satin or silk and is nicely embroidered. It's a family heirloom or it's hand-made or you can buy it anywhere, including Amazon. It's supposed to be six feet square and fit on four posts. The groom walks down the aisle before the bride and stands under the *huppa*, with his parents and hers. The rabbi may welcome him with a prayer. The bride comes down the aisle (I have never heard the musicians play "Here Comes the Bride" at a Jewish wedding) and stands, with her parents and bridesmaids to the groom's right. The bridesmaids, best man and ushers do not have to be Jewish under anybody's rules. Sometimes, under American custom, the bride's father escorts the bride down the aisle to a point a few feet from the *huppa* where the groom meets them and takes the bride. Everybody ends up under the *huppa*: the couple, the parents, the rabbi (or other officiant) and the person who's doing the videotape. The ushers and bridesmaid stand just off to each side. I'm not sure how all this works in a gay wedding ceremony. I'm sure you're allowed to improvise.

In the first part of the ceremony (called the *erusin*), the rabbi raises a goblet and says a prayer. He gives a cup to the groom who tastes and then holds if for the bride, affirming that, throughout life, they will share together the good, the bad, and the ugly.

When a Jewish man marries a Jewish woman he will put a ring

on her finger. Custom says it should be the index finger of the right hand, up to the second joint because there is a vein there which runs directly to the heart. Jewish law says that the ring must be a solid, unbroken circle of metal with no gems or stones, symbolizing the couple's unbroken union achieved through marriage. The groom, on putting the ring on the finger will say "Behold, thou are consecrated unto me with this ring according to the laws of Moses and Israel." Non-Jewish partners will not say that. In fact, truth be told, Susan and I had never heard of these customs and, as for the ring and the prayer at least, we wouldn't have observed them.

One much more observed custom, however, is that of the *ketubah* which is the marriage contract. It can be read aloud under the *huppa*. It recites the obligation of one partner to care for the other. It might actually go into excruciating detail, specifying, for example, the amount of money to be paid by one to the other in the event of divorce. It provides for security and protection and the rights to food, shelter, and conjugal relations. The punishment for breaking the contract used to be a two goats and a donkey kind of thing but, even today, *the ketubah* is enforceable in civil court in Israel. It could read a lot like a prenuptial agreement but, in the modern era, it focuses on customs that the couple will observe. You frame it and hang it on the wall, unless you want a fancy sculpture to go with it and that you order on-line. After the *ketubah* is read, the couple drinks a cup of wine.

During the second part of the ceremony (called the *nissuin*) the rabbi or cantor will recite seven blessings over another cup of wine. The ceremony concludes when the officiant wraps a glass in cloth, puts it on the floor, and the groom stomps on it (or, in more modern traditions, the couple breaks the glass together). Everybody then says *Mazel tov*! The roots of this particular custom are not clear. Some say it is to scare away the demons that would harm the couple. A very knowledgeable Jewish friend of mine says it's to celebrate the loss of virginity. More commonly, however, it is to remind everyone of the destruction of the temples, a reminder that joy must be tempered with the harsh reality of not only Jewish life but of those everywhere who suffer. The breaking ends the ceremony, the couple kisses (even though you don't often hear a rabbi say "you may now kiss the bride"), walk down the aisle, maybe the people throw a little rice and the couple leaves for a few minutes of solitude (called the *yichud*) before the party begins. They may snack if they have been observing the ancient custom of fasting all day.

The fun part is the celebration later. Dancing, drinking, eating, toasting – the whole *shtick*. You won't know most of the people at the wedding because they are friends of the parents – the so-called "wedding relatives." At some point, some groomsmen (or just friends) will sit the groom on a chair, lift him up and carry him around. At a modern wedding, they will also do the same for the bride. That's the chair dance. Hopefully, the lifters aren't totally hammered yet. It's embarrassing but not as bad as the custom of the dollar dance at Italian weddings where everybody pins money on the bridal couple while they have their dance. There will also be a time for dancing the Jewish national dance – the *hora* – to the Jewish national song "*Hava Nagila.*" Even if you've never seen it before, you should join in and be a good sport. It's just a little kick-kick-turn-center and out-kick-kick. Something like that. No big deal. For the kids, young and old, there might be a limbo song, maybe a bunny hop. At some point, the best man or woman makes a toast. You know the routine.

I shamelessly add the Judaic teachings on sex not only because they are interesting but also because every book should have some tit-illation in it. Sex is not considered sinful, shameful or for-procreation-only in Judaism. Desire is a perfectly good rationale for having sex. Lest you get the wrong idea, we are talking marital sex only. This is the spot for Rabbi Jonathan Gerard's joke about the Orthodox Jewish couple, preparing for their wedding at a final meeting with the rabbi:

The man asks: "Rabbi, is it true that men and women don't dance together?

"Yes," says the rabbi. "For modesty reasons, men and women dance separately."

So, at our wedding, I can't dance with my own wife?"

"No," answered the rabbi.

"Well, okay," says the man. "But what about sex?"

"Fine," replies the rabbi. "It is a *mitzvah* within the marriage, to have Jewish children."

"What about different positions?" asks the man.

"No problem," says the rabbi. It's a *mitzvah*.

"Women on top?" the man asks.

"Why not?" is the response. "Sex in a marriage is a *mitzvah*."

"Without clothes?"

"Of course! It's a *mitzvah*."

"Well, what about standing up?"

"Oh, NO. NO." Says the rabbi.

"Why not?" asks the man.

"Could lead to dancing."

Now, get this: the Talmud teaches that sex is the woman's right, not the man's. The husband has the duty to give his wife sex regularly and in a way that is pleasurable. The Talmud even legislates minimum frequency of conjugal communion. "Everyday for men of leisure who do not need to work, twice a week for laborers, once a week for ass-drivers, once every thirty days for camel drivers, and once every six months for sailors. No kidding. (*Mishna Ketubot* 5:6). I figured you might want a reference for that one.

The three basic rights of woman, by tradition, are food, clothing, and sex. Pause and repeat. The husband must also offer sex without the wife having to ask for it. That goes without saying. The wife may never be forced to have sex. Nor is sex supposed to be used by either spouse as a weapon. Nor may the couple have sex while drunk or quarreling. Nor may they have sex during the wife's menstrual period, which, by some Talmudic calculations, last 12 days.

Something tells me that many would also like a Biblical citation for this last set of regulations. Gen. 2:18, Exod. 21:10.

The *Hava Nagila* is, without doubt, the only song you can be sure will be sung at a Jewish wedding (and, for that matter, at most *Bar/Bat Mitzvahs*). It was one of the first Israeli folk songs in Hebrew. Here are the lyrics:

Hava nagila	*Let's rejoice*
Hava nagila	*Let's rejoice*
Hava nagila ve-nismeḥa	*Let's rejoice and be happy (repeat)*
Hava neranenah	*Let's sing*
Hava neranenah	*Let's sing*
Hava neranenah ve-nismeḥa	*Let's sing and be happy (repeat)*
Uru, uru aḥim!	*Awake, awake, my brothers!*
Uru aḥim be-lev sameaḥ	*Awake my brothers with a happy heart*
Uru aḥim, uru aḥim!	*Awake, my brothers, awake, my brothers!*
Be-lev sameaḥ	*With a happy heart (repeat four times)*

There's a dance that goes with it but you'll have to pick that up by yourself. So how come you've heard this before without ever having been to a Jewish feast? Because Hava Nagila has truly crossed the genre divide. Harry Belafonte put it on his Harry Belafonte at Carnegie Hall album and closed every concert for 15 years with it. Many, many others have recorded it, including, of all people, Glen Campbell in his Oscar-nominated True Grit album (You Tube has an instrumental version because he says he could never manage the words to sing it). But my paisano friend Connie Francis sang the hell out of it on her best-selling album of Jewish favorites. She had been singing the song for years in the Borscht Belt, sometimes known as the Catskills. When asked if she was Jewish, she would often answer: "I'm ten percent Jewish on my manager's side."

FUNERALS AND SITTING SHIVA

Jews don't do wakes. They don't do viewings of the deceased. They don't send flowers to surround the casket. Nor do they often do funeral services at the temple or synagogue. The service is usually held in a chapel at the funeral home, after which all who want to will go in procession to the cemetery. There is no requirement of a chapel service. The rabbi can do the service at the gravesite.

Here's how it works if there is a chapel service. The immediate family will arrive an hour early and sit in an anteroom to receive condolences from family and friends. The family comes out at the appointed time for the service. Usually, several psalms and a memorial prayer are read. It is the rabbi who will have discussed the deceased with the family prior to the service who usually gives the eulogy. The eulogy can range from the straightforward to the gut-wrenchingly hilarious. Other family members may also give eulogies or say a prayer. Ordinarily, the casket is closed to the public. When the service is over, pallbearers wheel the casket to the hearse, which then leads the procession to the cemetery.

At the cemetery, there are prayers and *kaddish* will be said if there is a *minyan* of ten Jewish men present. Loved ones then take a turn and each throws a shovelful of earth onto the casket. The family leaves when the casket is covered with earth.

In any event, the deceased is put into the ground with all deliberate speed. Under Jewish law, burial is supposed to occur within 24 hours of death. Like so much else in the Jewish religion, that's flexible. In addition, there are no burials on the sabbath or on the first day of festivals. Cremation is prohibited by the Orthodox and Conservative tradition as a defiling of the body. In addition, there are historical, cultural and spiritual arguments against it. Nonetheless, Jews, particularly Reform Jews, are increasingly cremating their dead. The cremated may even be buried in Jewish cemeteries.

Unlike the Christian manner of holding a wake before the funeral, the Jewish family and friends "sit *shiva*" for a number of days after the burial to mourn the dead. The family arrives at the *shiva* house from the cemetery, they wash their hands before entering the house, and the family observance begins.

Shiva means seven which is the traditional number of days that a family will sit because that's how long Joseph mourned for his father Jacob in Genesis. It commonly happens nowadays that a family will sit for only three days or even just one evening after the cemetery service. Immediate family will be there every night. Close friends will usually sit for more than one night. If a major holiday begins (*Rosh Hashanah, Yom Kippur, Pesach, Shavout or Sukkot*), the rest of the *shiva* is canceled. For the next ten days, the observant will not listen to music, radio or television; there will be no haircutting, no wearing of new clothes, no parties, weddings or dances. For the parents, the mourning is 12 months.

Here is what to expect when you visit a *shiva* house to pay what is called a *shiva* or condolence call. A pitcher of water near the door is meant to wash the impurities associated with death off your hands. Only the very observant will cover the mirrors in the *shiva* house. The point is that one is not supposed to pay attention to oneself at this tragic moment. Some traditionalists will still sit on low stools or crates and wear slippers or sneakers instead of leather shoes which is a sign of luxury or vain comfort. The family, according to tradition but not modern practice, should not shave or cut hair during *shiva*. You will note that many Jews, particularly Reform Jews, will not observe too many of these customs.

Unfortunately, I have had occasion to sit *shiva* many times. If I could capsulize the atmosphere, it's that of a subdued social occasion. The Christian wake has a social aspect to it also. With the deceased's body in the room, however, I always found the wake to be very somber, particularly if the wake is held at the funeral home where there is usually a receiving line before standing or kneeling in front of the casket. Sitting *shiva* is done in the home where the evidence of the deceased's life is all around. After you arrive, you'll greet the family and someone will immediately ask you if you've eaten.

If you want to send or take something to the *shiva* house, make it food. A fruit basket or cookies perhaps. Jews do not do flowers at the time of death. Talking and even laughing is often heard in a *shiva* house, particularly if people are talking about the deceased. Tradition has it that talk about the deceased is a comfort. Take your lead from the mourners: if they talk, you talk. Though the event may also be a chance to catch up with people, try to avoid spending the whole evening talking about yourself. There is an old Jewish saying: "Words from the heart go directly to the heart." Most of all, your simple presence brings solace.

There will be enormous amounts of food. Traditionally, the community makes a meal of condolence for the family. Now, the deli tray has taken over. Close friends or family will order deli trays from delis or caterers filled with meat, whitefish, lox, cheeses, and vegetables. And then there's the dessert tray. And the drinks. And everybody talks about how they have never seen a tray as fabulous as that one tonight. Unless you're really close, don't stay more than an hour.

At some point during the evening, you may hear someone say that a *minyan* is present. That means there are ten Jewish men present who can now say *Kaddish* which are the memorial prayers. Reform, Reconstructionist and even some Conservative Jews will count Jewish women to make the ten.

Nine months to a year after death, there is a ceremony at the gravesite to dedicate the tombstone. This custom is a 19th Century British and American creation. A cloth is draped over the monument. A rabbi says a eulogy and a *minyan* will lead the prayers, if available. The stone is then unveiled. A memorial service for the dead is called the *yiskor*. It's held four times a year, during *Passover, Shavous, Sukkot, and Yom Kippur. Yahrzeit* is the yearly anniversary of death. Often, Jews will go to synagogue or light a candle in the home on *yahrzeit*.

CHAPTER 6

HOW YOUR FOOD CHOICE CAN GIVE YOU AWAY; LOVING JEWISH FOOD AND HATING *TRAYF*

WHEN MY JEWISH wife Susan went to my Italian Aunt Adriana's house, she ate the eggplant parmesan, the braciole, the cauliflower fritters, and the pasta with all the zest of a starving child. My Aunt, needless to say, was thrilled. "You know," said she, "you'd think Susan was an Italian girl." Bada-boom. Success. Acceptance. All you have to do is eat well and a lot. Susan comes by her enthusiasm honestly. Jews and Italians and Greeks and other Mediterranean types have a mutual affinity and enthusiasm for good food and an atmosphere of celebration while preparing the food and eating it. It's a time of family, friendship and community. In Jewish life, most celebrations or key moments in life involve food – a key symbol of Jewish culture. This is good. Food makes you feel better. Even the Bible says so: when Moses and the elders went up the mountain, "they saw the God of Israel, and they beheld Godhood, and they ate and drank." (Ex. 24:10-11).

My initiation into good Jewish food was at the top of the line – the New York Jewish delicatessen. Bagels as they were meant to be, hot and lean pastrami, meat and potato *knishes*, *kishke*, the fat, succulent pickles, egg creams and black-and-white cookies. Jewish food, to me, was lunch food. It took a long time before I experienced what Jews eat for dinner, which is what really opened me to the variety and richness of Jewish food. Even from the beginning, though, I always thought Jewish food had more character than standard fare. As Steve Allen once said: "Words like lox, herring, chopped liver, chicken soup and *matzah* are inherently more amusing than trout, bass, lamb stew, vegetable soup and whole wheat bread."

When you think about it, it's a wonder there is such a thing as Jewish food. Chinese food comes from China. Italian food comes from Italy. Where does Jewish food come from? The fact is that Jewish food has followed the Jews as they were scattered throughout history in various corners of the world. The set of dietary laws is called the *kashrut* and it is written that the laws were given to Moses on Mt. Sinai. Even if it wasn't that long ago, the *kashrut* has been passed down through the ages from the *Torah* (Levitticus and Deuteronomy) to everything else. It says that most mammals, fish and birds are OK but if the animal doesn't eat meat, like pigs and shellfish, they are forbidden. Anything not slaughtered according to kosher laws is also forbidden. Any mixing of meat and dairy is also forbidden. Why, you ask? Nobody really knows, except to say that they are tests of obedience. Some scholars say there are other reasons, including one of the big ones, Maimonides, who says kosher food is better for your health. I'll leave it to you to continue the research on that question. I eat everything.

Within these prohibitions, Jewish food has adapted to its surroundings. In the U.S. today, it is the food of the East European Jews, the *Ashkenazim*, who came here around the turn of the last century, that dominates the modern Jewish menu. The *Sephardim* dishes reflect the African influence, like couscous, filo pastry and *kibbeh*.

It is not true that everything Jewish is overcooked, unless, of course, you were in my mother-in-law's house. Even so, what's so bad about dry turkey? It's not true that Jews never eat spicy food. It's just that most are on low-salt diets. It is also not true that Jews eat only Jewish food. In fact, my experience is that Jews are obsessed with Chinese food.

Chicken Matzah Ball Soup

Once you get beyond bagels and chicken soup, though, Jewish food is a mystery to most gentiles. We seem to think, first, that being Jewish means you can't eat anything good or that if it's good, it can't be kosher. Wrong. Jews eat pasta and chocolate and most everything else that makes life worth living. Second, we think that most Jews observe the dietary laws. Wrong again. Not everybody separates the meat and the dairy or abstains from shellfish. On the other hand, because of a kosher or near-kosher upbringing, many Jews have simply not acquired a taste for certain common foods, like ham, bacon, or mayonnaise.

What does it Mean to "Keep *Kosher?*"

Orthodox and more traditional Jewish families will "keep *kosher*." That means that they will eat and prepare food according to the Jewish law – the *kashrut* that sets out the code of *kosher* food. This means, for example, that you do not eat dairy and meat at the same meal. No cheeseburgers. No milkshakes with your meat. Three to six hours must pass before switching from one to the other. You don't eat pork, hare, camel, or shellfish or any fish that doesn't have fins or scales. Meat must be slaughtered according to *kosher* ritual (e.g. the blood must all be drained before eating), so meat must be purchased at a *kosher* butcher. Some *kosher* products carry a little "*k*" on the package to indicate rabbinical supervision of the making of the product. I checked on this and, it's true, there's a niche for rabbis who supervise food preparation and butchering. They have a special name and belong to a service union, albeit the Orthodox Union. Other products will be labeled *pareve* which they are OK to eat because they have no meat, dairy, pork or shellfish ingredients. No grape products made by gentiles can be taken (try not to mention that as everyone drinks the fourth cup of wine at Passover). If you want to get really technical, no sciatic nerve or adjoining blood vessels can be eaten.

You might be amazed (as I once was) to know that a *kosher* home will have two sets of dishes, flatware, and pots and pans to keep the dairy and the meat separate. They will use separate sponges and dish-towels for cleaning, and sometimes separate can openers, separate sinks for washing and separate place mats. If you use a dishwasher, separate racks are used for meat and dairy unless you run the machine empty once before reloading. Again, it's not clear why Jewish law has these requirements but in Exodus and Deuteronomy, the phrase "you shall not boil a kid in its mother's milk" is repeated five times. I guess that pretty much settles it.

I choose to focus on cleanliness as the rationale for these rules. Cooking and eating milk and dairy together is seen as not clean. What if it's organic and gluten-free? Unclean food is called *treyf* because it was not slaughtered or prepared according to Jewish law and is therefore unfit to be eaten. The food of almost any nationality can be *kosher*. *Kosher* Chinese food is very popular in some places. The *kosher* refers not to the style of food but rather to the method of preparation.

The Hall of Fame of Jewish Foods

The basic and most common Friday night Sabbath dinner will consist of the bread *challah*, chicken soup, a brisket of beef or roasted chicken and a *kugel*, which is a kind of noodle pudding in casserole. There is no law, however, that says that has to be the menu. In fact, Jewish cooks have become specialists of fusion cookery which combines the best of traditional Jewish food and the most *nouveau* of all the polyglot *nouveaux*. Because all Jews can eat fish with scales, I'm told of the Hasidic (very Orthodox) wedding that featured a sushi bar and the Jewish restaurant that puts their salmon casserole right up front.

So, here is my highly opinionated list of great Jewish foods, in alphabetical order.

Bagel　　　You know what this is. It's just not easy to find good ones. Bagels were adopted in America, kind of like hot dogs. Don't even bother trying to find good ones in Europe or anyplace else except maybe Israel. It used to be that you only had to decide what you wanted on your bagel, like poppy seeds or sesame seed. Now, they have 57 different flavors, including mint chocolate chip. Those aren't real bagels, just like pineapples don't really go on a pizza. A real bagel is soft and warm, with a crispy, crackly outside and a spongy inside. Many people like it toasted which is the great equalizer among pretty much all bagels. With lox, cream cheese, tomato, herring, whitefish or all of the above, it is an American masterpiece.

Bialy	A bialy is like a bagel but it's not. It's round but with no hole. It has a depressed middle that is filled with onions, seeds, or other stuff. It's baked and should be eaten fresh from the oven. Go into a Jewish deli in New York or, maybe, South Florida sometime and order "an everything bialy with a *schmear* and lox." Do it soon, they're disappearing.
Borsht	This is a beet soup, served hot or cold (I prefer hot) and sometimes with sour cream.
Brisket	A brisket of beef is a staple for holiday meals. Cooked sometimes like a stew for hours and hours and sliced thinly with its own gravy on top. It's a real taste treat. Never ask for a piece of rare, medium rare, or even medium brisket. There is no such thing as an over-cooked brisket.
Challah	(Don't pronounce the "c" and go heavy on the first "h"; you can't pronounce this word without beginning to spit). This is great Jewish bread. It's a braided egg bread that should be light and sweet and golden. Common on the Sabbath and all holidays. The normal meal always begins with the breaking of bread. On *Rosh Hashanah*, use the round-shaped loaf (which symbolizes eternal life). It makes great French toast.

Challah

Chicken soup Any number of variations and additions. It's known universally as a remedy for all that ails you. Arthur Naiman calls chicken soup an ancient miracle drug. "The only ailment it can't cure," he says, "is neurotic dependence on one's mother."

Chopped liver You know this one too. It's like a pate and it's better with chicken than with beef liver.

Gefiltefish This is a fish cake or fish loaf. It is made with a variety of deboned fish (carp, whitefish or pike), mixed with eggs, onions, pepper, carrots, and other seasonings, held together with *matzah* and egg and ground into a loaf by you or the fishmonger who sells it (not so easy to find). It is served with horseradish and eaten at Friday night dinner (to encourage fertility, as the legend goes) and on holidays. It's an acquired taste.

Kishka	Literally, this is beef or fowl "casings" or intestines. Stuff the intestines with good stuff, like matzo meal, chopped carrots and onions or buckwheat. Oil it up and then roast it or fry it. It's so much better fried. Isn't everything? Despite its description, it's really good. The word is sometimes used to refer to "guts," as in "don't get your *kishkas* in an uproar."
Knish	(pronounce both the "k" and the "h"). This is one of the foods that got me started on Jewish food. It's a potato and sour dumpling baked with stuffing: meat, cheese or just more potato. Usually, it comes out rectangular in shape. It's a snack or an appetizer. It's also great street food (mostly in New York, where they put mustard on the inside).
Kugel	This is a noodle or potato pudding that looks more like a quiche or a casserole. Usually a side dish but I have noticed that a lot of Jews would kill for a good *kugel*. Made with noodles, onions or fruits in an egg-based pudding. It can be either sweet with raisins and sour cream or savory with onions or eggs. This is where you get your carbs.
Knaidlach	*Matzah* balls made with matzah meal and eggs and other stuff, like parsley and pepper. Common at Passover.
Kreplach	This is kind of like ravioli. It's a dumpling that contains meat or cheese. It's usually served in soup.
Latkes	These are the famous potato pancakes that are served most commonly at *Chanukah*. They are fried in oil and served with applesauce or sour cream. Don't use syrup. It's eaten at *Chanukah* because it burns for eight days when lit (I've never tried that).
Lox	Lox is a quintessential Jewish food. It is smoked

	salmon (the Nova variation of lox is smoked; regular lox are cold-cured), eaten salted or unsalted. Very popular at Sunday brunch. It's also very expensive but when you put it on a bagel with cream cheese, you're living high.
Matzo	(or *matzah*) This is unleavened bread. In its unvarnished form, it's a long, thin, relatively tasteless cracker. Combined with other ingredients, it's shaped into balls and put into the number one Jewish remedy – chicken soup. Then it's called *matzo* ball soup or, as some prefer, penicillin. Sometimes it's broken up, mixed with egg, soaked and fried to become *matzo brei*.
Pastrami	Along with corned beef, this is the #1 Jewish sandwich. You want the pastrami in long, lean slices. You eat it on rye bread with mustard. On white bread or with mayonnaise is a *shonda* – a shame.
Stuffed cabbage	This was very common in the Old Country (Eastern Europe) where it was known as *holishkes*, meaning cabbage stuffed with meatballs in a tomato-based sweet and sour sauce.
Tsimmes	A sweet stew of mixed vegetables, usually with carrots, sweet potatoes and prunes. Popular at *Rosh Hashanah*. Sometimes, the word is used to mean a big fuss: "Don't make such a *tsimmes* about it!"

Popular Jewish Baked Goods and Pastries

Babka	This is sweet, buttered bread – cake, really. Its name is close to the Polish word for grandmother because, in its Eastern European countries of origin, it was the grandmothers who made it. It usually has swirls of chocolate or cinnamon running through it. Or it can just plain be dipped in chocolate. I had some

recently that was filled with pistachios and cream. To die for.

Blintzes This is a very traditional *Ashkenazi* Jewish dish that is very similar to *blinis* which are historically an Eastern Slavic dish. *Blintzes* were brought to the U.S. by the Eastern European Jews and adapted somewhat to American tastes. So what is it, you ask? It's a thin pancake that will be stuffed with something. I've included it in this section because, when stuffed with cherries or strawberries or some other fruit, it's definitely dessert. They are, however, often stuffed with cheese and can be served anytime. It's another variation of the Jewish crepe.

Hamantashen These are the most delicious pastries, always eaten on the feast of *purim* but you can definitely sneak some at other times if you know a good Jewish deli. The cookie dough is folded into a neat triangle (symbolic of the villian Haman's ear) and then filled with good stuff– from poppy seeds, to apricots, prunes, even caramel apple filling.

Kichel	This is a light cookie to dunk in the coffee. It's actually rolled in sugar and baked crispy on the outside, soft on the inside, with or without chocolate chips. Usually they're shaped into little bow-ties. Very commonly served at *Bar/Bat Mitzvahs*.
Rugelach	These little cookies would probably win the prize as the number one Jewish dessert. They're a buttery and flaky rolled pastry. Not a cookie. They are shaped and taste like a small *croissant*. They are, however, much richer and much more varied. They can range from chocolate-covered to nut rolls with fillings like marzipan, poppy seeds, fruit preserves, etc.
Macaroons	Like so many pastries popular with Jewish families, macaroons aren't really Jewish. Like black-and-white cookies or lemon squares. But they've been adopted. They are small cookies, particularly popular at Passover because they aren't made with flour or leavening. They are usually made with ground almonds or coconuts or other nuts. They may have a chocolate coating or a cream filling. They're very rich but delicious.
mandelbrot	Mandel bread looks and tastes a lot like Italian *biscotti*. It's an *Ashkenazi* Jewish dessert dating back to the 19th Century. They are twice baked so as to make them crunchier. They last a long time (because most of the moisture has been baked out) and they are great for dipping. Though I can't prove it, I'm thinking that Jews in northern Italy took the biscotti north to Austria, changed its name and called it their own. Happy to share.

Rugelach

CHAPTER 7

CONVINCING JEWS THAT YOU ARE NOT ANTI-SEMITIC: THE ULTIMATE LOSING BATTLE

THIS IS A tricky issue. It's a little like trying to convince African-Americans that you, if you're white, are not racist. There's a reason why the analogy holds up. Both Jews and African-Americans have suffered from centuries of racism and ethnic hatred. Both were enslaved. Both have been subject to endless and oppressive stereotyping. The track record of happy and peaceful co-existence is not good. So, those of us who are neither Jewish nor African-American will just have to understand why it is that saying "some of my best friends are..." does not absolve you of the sins of your forbearers.

Even twenty years into the new millennium, many Jews see themselves as outsiders to mainstream society and no amount of counterpoint is going to convince them otherwise. That this country is as multicultural as it has ever been and that Jews are well integrated at every level of society doesn't matter. Nor does it matter that being

Jewish sometimes isn't even noticed by gentiles. "We just don't think that way anymore" is a gentile protest that is likely to fall upon deaf Jewish ears. The Holocaust wasn't that many years ago. Jews will tell you that if you scratch the surface many of those anti-Semitic feelings are still there. Every time a Jewish tombstone gets defaced or a synagogue gets attacked or a Jewish kid gets called the "k" word, history rears its head again. Most of my own post-modern Jewish friends still would not consider making a major decision like where to live, where to work, or where to go to school without counting the Jews. My own wife checks out the number of Jews in the phone book in practically every town we visit from Peoria to Saigon.

I've also noticed that some of the occasional cultural isolation comes from a distrust of gentiles because they are so different. This comes from Philip Weiss, about WASPS: "We regard WASPS with considerable mistrust. They were cold and aloof: they had bad taste. We made fun of their clothes and mindlessness. They had wooden relationships with their children. They were responsible for violent, idiotic misadventures like Vietnam and Bosnia and riding motorboats around at night."

That thought reflects as exaggerated and stereotypical a view as one would hear going the other way from an anti-Semite. My gentile reactions are, first, not all gentiles are WASPS. This is something I have struggled with ever since I entered the Jewish sectors of my life: the failure of most Jews I know to make important non-Jewish cultural distinctions. There is a tendency to see us as all the same: Protestants, Catholics, Irish, Poles, what have you. I will admit to seeing a widespread appreciation of Italians among my Jewish friends and family since, as Mediterranean types, we are almost *landsmen*. And just for the historical record, the primary architect of the Vietnam War was Henry Kissinger - a Jew. But I got Weiss' idea. It's funny and not meant to be taken literally. I have to keep reminding myself of that when I'm feeling defensive around Jews. And then I wonder, "does their relationship with me make them put the stereotypes aside or do they need to keep them as a way of giving order to life?" We need to understand

Jewish caution. Europe in the 20's, even 30's was much like America today in that anti-Semitic ideas were given free rein in public. Today, we see dramatic increases in the number of anti-Semitic incidents in many parts of the world. For those reasons, we shouldn't be surprised that, according to various studies, most Jews still think anti-Semitism to be a serious problem.

Having said that, I have nonetheless noticed some particularities to the Jewish distrust of gentiles that could be of use in attempting to bridge the cultural divide. When I first started seeing Susan seriously, I tried to ingratiate myself to her family. I learned a lot of things that, hopefully, you have now learned from this book – culture, history, religion, festivals, etc. The expectations of me were not high. As long as I was respectful at dinner and at *Bar Mitzvahs* and while sitting *shiva*, I was OK. These are modern, non-Orthodox Jews, to whom marriage to a gentile is no longer such a big deal, although still a bit of a disappointment. Many family members went out of their way to communicate with me, like the cousin who always talked to me about home repairs because he assumed all gentiles are handy.

I tried not to overdo it and let people get used to me gradually. I advise no showing off of how much you know about Judaism, no constant favorable comparisons of Judaism with Christianity, no dyeing your blonde hair brown, no trying too hard. Relax but be on your good behavior. When you're thinking of saying something risky, try to hold off until people know you better. Don't say things like "Jews are…" or "you Jews." And don't drink too much. On that point, the first drink is fine. The second drink will be noticed. Three drinks and it's "I'm not saying he's got a drinking problem, but…." I once asked for a glass of scotch at Cousin Alan's house. That set off this frantic search for booze in the house. I was immediately sorry but it was too late. Behind the good napkins and the tablecloths, a shelf was emptied: a couple of bottles of super-sweet wine, a dusty, old, unopened bottle of Bailey's Irish Cream, schnapps and a bottle of whiskey that was last used at little Kenny's *bris*. I asked Susan what one is most likely to find in a typical Jewish liquor cabinet. She sneered at my stupid question and said "Jewish liquor cabinet is an oxymoron." That said, I have a number of Jewish friends who stock good wine and scotch. It just depends.

Little by little, show how comfortable you're becoming with Jewishness. Wear the *yarmulke* in temple (only if you're male and don't even do that if the family doesn't) and pay attention to the prayers being recited in Hebrew, which you happen not to speak (older Catholics should just make believe they are in church in the days before the Latin was changed to English). Spice up your conversation a little. Use a few Jewish words here and there, use some old family sayings to illustrate your point, show a little aggravation. Do little but noticeable things: eat a second helping, pick up a check once in awhile, do the hugging thing. And don't drink too much. Many years ago, at a first meeting, I kissed a future uncle-in-law on the cheek, without thinking, and after my two drinks. They're still talking about it.

Eventually, it will be reported to you that somebody important in the family said publicly: such a nice boy (girl); too bad he (she) isn't Jewish." This is progress. When cousin Harry says "Are you sure you're not Jewish?" this is as close as you're going to get.

If a mixed marriage is in the offing, the ante is upped. Only Orthodox or extremely Conservative families will challenge the Jewish son or daughter and try to stop the marriage. That is so *depasse'*. Then there is the question of converting to Judaism. In my case, my mother-in-law wanted me to convert and, in fact, she tried to bribe me. When I continued to respectfully decline, she got heavy with me and threatened me. Since I'm Italian, she figured I could relate to the threat that she would "take out a contract" on me. I'm not making this stuff up. I'm not that kind of Italian, so it didn't bother me and she was just upset. As sweet and generous as she was (our relationship improved enormously), she would have no idea on how to take a contract out on anybody.

Eventually, it all blew over, we got married, and the process of acceptance continued apace. Jews know that over 50% of all Jews intermarry with gentiles, so they fear that American Jewry will be melted away into the melting pot. I totally understand this reluctance to accept assimilation. In my family, every time we did something very non-Jewish, the Jewish part of the family accepted it but had something-not-too-subtle to say. I'll never forget my mother-in-law walking into our house and seeing, for the first time in her daughter's house, a Christmas tree in the corner. "That tree," says she, "is responsible for the killing of thousands of Jews." She always made her point but, within days, she was putting presents under the tree herself.

That reluctance around assimilation is aggravated by the collective Jewish memory of the Holocaust and the gentile world's reaction to it. Despite all the examples of the heroic efforts of many non-Jews to save Jews from deportation, the overriding fact is that most governments were indifferent to the plight of the Jews (see the history section and, in particular, the story of the cruise liner St. Louis). The specter of the Holocaust is often raised by Jews, particularly emanating from Israel, accusing some view as being "Nazi-like." It's anxiety. None can call it neurotic anxiety given the sordid history of the treatment of the Jews throughout the recorded past.

There is an evolution to Jewish stereotypes. The more modern ones, often media-induced, are just as virulent as the old ones. The JAP (Jewish-American princess) stereotype is a good example. It's acceptable to many gentiles to use the term JAP to refer to any Jewish woman whom they perceive to be "bitchy, spoiled, materialistic or frigid." The term JAP is just as offensive to most Jewish females as the n-word is to African-Americans. Yet, somehow, popular culture seems to allow the term in polite conversation. As an Italian-American of primarily Sicilian origin, I have often felt insulted by the stigmata of the mafia. Many of my *paisanos* wear the association with pride. I, on the other hand, feel unjustly maligned. So much about the mafia is portrayed as almost cute, that many people think they are complimenting you as some kind of tough guy. To me, it's repulsive. The Poles suffer from being called stupid; the Irish are called a bunch of drunks, the English are uptight and anal retentive. These stereotypes are all offensive. The only question is one of degree.

So you want to Convert to Judaism?

First of all, Jews don't recruit. No Jewish missionaries, no rabbis leading a crusade to, say, El Paso. Some temples do not even have a website, nor is there any internet presence at all so there is obviously no attempt to increase the size of the congregation. In fact, the more Orthodox the Jew, the less likely the convert will be accepted. Syrian Jews (including the communities in New York and New Jersey) still do not accept and will ostracize anyone who marries a convert. The more Reform-minded Jews are much more accepting.

Many mixed marriages result in the conversion of one spouse to Judaism. Others convert simply because they want to be Jewish. The 2014 Religious Landscape Study of the Pew Research Center found that fully 17% or 1 in 6 Jews were raised in another religion and converted to Judaism. For those who would attempt to cross the ethnic divide and become "Jews by choice," I will mention a few of the basics about the process, with a bow to *The Jewish Home Advisor*.

But first a warning: ask any Jew and they will tell you that the converts can be the most difficult. If I've seen it once, I've seen it seven or eight times that the convert winds up being more religiously Jewish than anybody. Maybe they measure the success of their conversion by how totally Judaism takes over their life: meticulous faithfulness to the Sabbath, volunteering for important roles at the temple, pains taken to separate the meat from the dairy and even frequency of trips to Israel – just to name a few symptoms of the pathology. As one rabbi put it, "our imports are better than our exports." In my view, a truly successful conversion asks only for faith in and respect for Jewish teaching and observance of the basic traditions and ceremonies. The kind of lock-step obsession that seems to overtake some converts is not necessary. I have convert friends who have even changed their gentile first name to a Jewish name. I'm sure that they have the best chance of being completely accepted into the Jewish community. All I know is that whenever I hear one of them mentioned by name, it's always "Joe Jones – he converted."

Historically, converts were never easily accepted into Judaism.

Rabbis typically discouraged potential converts. Today, people who are converting are required to convince the rabbi that the conversion is a sincere one and that Judaism is being embraced in all its essential forms. Those who seek converts as a means of increasing the Jewish population are often accused of having a "market place" approach to religion, particularly in America, where the there are so many religions, there is often competition with each other for converts. On the other hand, converting a spouse to Judaism often reactivates the already Jewish spouse's interest – kind of a two-for-one deal.

Orthodox and Conservative Judaism hold that, based on *Talmudic* law, the child of a Jewish mother and a gentile father is considered Jewish. The child of a Jewish father and a gentile mother, however, must convert. There is no Jewish concept that considers such a child to be "half-Jewish." You're Jewish or you aren't. Even if you aren't observant, even if you convert to something else, you're still Jewish if your mother was.

Reform and Reconstructing Judaism consider the child in a mixed marriage to be Jewish if the parents want the child to be raised Jewish. So no formal conversion is required.

Those who actually wish to go through the conversion process have to study Jewish beliefs, prayers and rituals for from six months to one year. Then notices are printed in a Jewish court (the *bet din*) seeking to be accepted as a candidate. Being an acceptable candidate requires a greater commitment to Judaism than just to grant the partners to the marriage their marriage wish. A friend of mine was told that her significant other had to do the study with her to avoid the convert being "more Jewish than the Jew." The bad news, for adult males converting to Orthodox or Conservative Judaism is that they must be circumcised – the dreaded *bris*. The good news is that Reform Judaism does not require circumcision. Nor does Reform require immersion in the *mikvah*, which is a ritual bath with three witnesses. In any event, the final stage is an appearance before the *bet din*, which is a formal declaration of the acceptance of and by Judaism, usually made during a service at the temple.

I hope you understand what I meant when I titled this chapter. It has been about proving you are not anti-Semitic even though it's "the ultimate losing battle." There will always be an invisible barrier, however lean, between the well-meaning gentile and the Jewish family. There is a barrier simply because Jews know that most gentiles do not know Jewish history, customs or values. Jews know that every gentile needs to be educated about the discrimination that Jews have suffered – the kind of education that all Jewish children, to one degree or another, are raised with. Jews know that very few gentiles will care to learn in detail what it means to be Jewish and that they will be satisfied with learning a few of the most spectacular Jewish expressions that, somehow, seem to say it all. So, that's hopefully why you bought this book.

I'm not sure how many of your questions I have answered but, as I said in the beginning, who needs answers anyway? If you're a gentile and you're going to be involved in Jewish life, just keep your sense of humor. It's all pretty funny when you think about it. Learn some words, read a little about the holidays and the religion, have seconds on the food. If you've absorbed even half of what I have tried to explore with you, you will be pleasantly surprised by your reception in the Jewish community (remember, don't be a show-off). It won't be long before somebody Jewish will say to you: "Funny, you don't look Jewish." Ba-da boom.

IF YOU WANT MORE...

Eckstein, Rabbi Yechiel, "What Christians Should Know About Jews and Judaism." (Word Books, 1984)

Feldman, Rabbi Abraham J.,"The American Jew." (Greenwood Press, 1979)

Klenicki, Leon and Wigoder, Geoffrey (eds.) " A Dictionary of the Jewish Christian Dialogue," (Stimulus Books, 1984)

Kolatch, Alfred J., "The Jewish Home Advisor," (Jonathan David, New York, 1990); Kolatch, Alfrred J., "The Second Jewish Book of Why," (Jonathan David, New York, 1985)

Naiman, Arthur, "Every Goy's Guide to Common Jewish Expressions," (Ballantine Books, New York, 1985)

Rosten, Leo, "Joys of Yiddish" (Penguin Random House, 2003)

Katz, Molly, "Jewish as a Second Language," (Workman Publishing, 1991)

Szlakmann, Charles, "Judaism for Beginners," (Writers and Readers Publishing, Inc. New York, 1990)

Drucker,Malka. "The Family Treasury of Jewish Holidavs" (Little Brown, 1994)

Judaism 101 - wwwJewfaq.org

Olitzky, Kerry M. and Isaacs, Ronald H., "The Second How to Handbook for Jewish Living," (KYAV Publlishing, 1996)

Telushkin, Rbbi Joseph, "<u>Jewish Humor: What the Best Jewish Jokes Say about the Jews,</u>" (Morrow and Co, Inc., New York, 1996)

Kertzer, Rabbi Morris, "<u>What is a Jew?</u>" (Collier Books, 1978)

David, Jay, "<u>Growing Up Jewish,</u>" (Avon Books, New York, 1996)

CPSIA information can be obtained
at www.ICGtesting.com
Printed in the USA
BVHW020152030521
606318BV00018B/1057